Cecil Beaton

WAR PHOTOGRAPHS 1939-45

FOREWORD BY PETER QUENNELL

INTRODUCTION BY GAIL BUCKLAND

Imperial War Museum
JANE'S

First published in 1981 by the Imperial War Museum
Lambeth Road, London SE1 6HZ
and Jane's Publishing Company Ltd
238 City Road, London EC1V 2PU

ISBN 0 7106 0136 0

Designed by Herbert and Mafalda Spencer
Text set by D. P. Media Limited, Hitchin, Hertfordshire
Made and printed in Italy by Arnoldo Mondadori Editore, Verona

Frontispiece: Cecil Beaton in the Western Desert, 1942

Cecil Beaton: War Photographs 1939-45

Contents

Page 6 Acknowledgements
     7 Foreword
     8 Author's Note
     9 Introduction
    34 References

The Home Front

The Middle East

Burma and India

China

Notes on the Photographs
The Photographs Division of the Ministry of Information
The Collections
Books by Cecil Beaton about the War Years

Acknowledgements

The Imperial War Museum would like to acknowledge the cooperation of Sotheby's Belgravia in the production of this book. The generosity of the Director responsible for photographic material, Philippe Garner, in allowing unlimited access to the Beaton archive and in placing darkroom facilities at the Museum's disposal, is greatly appreciated. The following plates are reproduced by courtesy of Sotheby's: the frontispiece portrait of Cecil Beaton in uniform, which also appears on the dust-jacket; in the Home Front section, 1 to 3, 5 to 25, 30 to 44, 46 to 52, 54 to 56; and in the Middle East section, 82.

The photographs of Buckingham Palace (4) and of the Royal Family at Windsor (53) are reproduced by courtesy of Miss Eileen Hose, formerly personal secretary to Sir Cecil Beaton.

The Museum is grateful to Mr Charles Gibbs-Smith and Mrs Barbara Langston for advice and information about the organisation of the photographs of the Ministry of Information in which they served during the Second World War. Thanks are also due to the Public Record Office for access to official documents and to the Central Office of Information.

For permission to quote from Cecil Beaton's published writings the Imperial War Museum and Jane's would like to thank B T Batsford Ltd, William Collins Ltd, Hutchinson & Co Ltd, Her Majesty's Stationery Office, Doubleday & Co Ltd, Oxford University Press and Weidenfeld & Nicolson Ltd.

Foreword

I first came to know Cecil Beaton, as he deserved to be known, at the beginning of the Second World War, when our friend, the brilliant, ill-fated Charles Fry, a young and enterprising London publisher, suggested we should collaborate on a book of photographs and commentaries, for which he himself supplied an ingenious title. *Time Exposure* appeared in May 1941; and, during its preparation I was able to observe Cecil, who, in the mid-1920s, I had seen as an impassioned party-goer, seldom out of some splendid fancy-dress, from a very different point of view. I became aware that he was a remarkably hard-working man, a dedicated professional, sharply attentive to the smallest details of every image his camera produced. He thought little, I discovered, of leaving his bed between 5 and 6 am rather than leave a piece of work unfinished, and refused to take advantage either of his well-established reputation or of his natural facility.

At the same time, despite his indomitable panache and the air of intransigent dandyism that, as a means of both offence and defence, he would now and then assume, where his own imaginative work was concerned he was an extremely modest character, always anxious to learn and ready to welcome advice if he thought it worth taking. Thus, in middle age, because he wished to improve his draughtsmanship, he cheerfully painted and drew among the youthful students of the Slade School; and, when he used his pen, he would often submit his manuscripts, for correction and revision, to a more experienced writer.

The Second World War offered him a creative challenge that he immediately accepted; and I think myself, much as I admire many of his earlier and later works, that his war photographs, from his tragic and pathetic pictures of bombed London to his dramatic records of the North African campaign and his impressions, accompanied by some exquisite Chinese landscapes, of the struggle in the Far East, are probably his finest efforts. Here his problem was how to commemorate the brutal facts of twentieth-century history, yet simultaneously produce a composition that satisfied his own aesthetic sense of style. He succeeded again and again. He possessed not only unfailing technical skill, but an artist's vision of the life around him. His eye was wonderfully keen – a painter's eye behind a modern camera; and throughout his career, but especially during the war years, he employed it with magnificent results.

PETER QUENNELL

Author's Note

Jane Carmichael, Assistant Keeper of the Department of Photographs, has studied Cecil Beaton's war activities in depth and gave me access to all her research. Her assistance and guidance through the photographic collections both at the Imperial War Museum and Sotheby's Belgravia is sincerely appreciated. She wrote the captions to the photographs and the introductions to each picture section and these are excellent complements to the text.

Eileen Hose, personal secretary to Cecil Beaton for many years and his literary executor, has, as always, helped and encouraged me in every way. Hugo Vickers, Cecil Beaton's biographer, graciously permitted me to see papers and books in his possession. Charles Craig, Senior Lecturer, Faculty of Art and Photography, Harrow College of Higher Education, is writing a thesis on war photography and shared his ideas on the subject with me. Margaret Wagstaff of Sotheby's made certain that hundreds of Cecil Beaton's negatives were contact printed promptly by their fine photographers.

The staff of the Imperial War Museum has made by work rewarding and enjoyable. I should like to thank Dr Christopher Dowling, Keeper of the Department of Education and Publications; Mr Robert Crawford, Assistant Director and Keeper of the Department of Photographs; Angela Godwin, Deputy Keeper of the Department of Education and Publications; the staff of the Photographic Library; and the Museum's photographers, who produced new prints of the highest quality from Cecil Beaton's negatives.

It was a pleasure to work with Herbert Spencer on the design of the book. His layout has preserved the dignity and beauty of the photographs.

Introduction

experience of photographer
see pics in museum

CB at ww1

Prologue

Yesterday I went to the Imperial War Museum, not my favourite place, to see the collection of photographs that I had taken during the war for the Ministry of Information. They have all been put into over thirty albums and, to my amazement, I find there are thirty or forty thousand of them. [Beaton has greatly exaggerated the total. In fact there are approximately 7,000 photographs in the Museum's collection.]

It was an extraordinary experience to relive those war years; so much of it had been forgotten, and most of the people are now dead; the Western Front, where at least three hundred of my pictures were unaccountably lost, Burma, India, China. It was fascinating to see the scenes in old Imperial Simla, the rickshaws drawn by uniformed servants, the grandeur of the houses, the men on leave swigging beer, and to wonder how I had been able to 'frat' with such unfamiliar types. The horrible war had taken me to beautiful landscapes I might not otherwise have seen. I had not realized that I had taken so many documentary pictures, some of purely technical interest. Looking at them today, I spotted ideas that are now 'accepted', but which, thirty years ago, were before their time. The sheer amount of work I had done confounded me.

It was a thrilling but upsetting morning, for I felt that I was dead and that the people were speaking of me in the past. 'The greatest collection by one person of any subject in our museum.'

I went out into the grey dreariness of Lambeth today. It has been a particularly revolting week with strikes, power cuts and epidemics. Despite the dark grey skies I was buoyant and would not believe that my life had lost any of its old fire and zest.[1]

So ends Cecil Beaton's last published diary. In his final years he often recalled the photographs he took during the Second World War and tried to remember how he had made these pictures of peasants and soldiers, war wounded, and shell-shattered buildings. He once told me that he thought they were, perhaps, the most serious work he had ever done. And yet he added, with a most searching look in his eye, that he did not know from what part of himself they came. Before and after the Second World War he concentrated on creating a fantasy world: women posed against shimmering tin foil and surrealistic back-drops; costumes and sets for theatrical productions; pictures of matinée idols, Hollywood stars and the splendour of royalty. He made high fashion and high society part of a dream only a few could otherwise share.

Photographing a world which seemed bent on self-destruction challenged Beaton as a man and as an artist as never before and never again. The photographs he took at home and abroad in the period from 1940 to 1944 confirm that a major change took place in Cecil Beaton. How well he saw, not only what he saw, is the subject of this book.

In 1974 Cecil Beaton and I collaborated on *The Magic Image*, an extensively illustrated anthology of the work of major photographers throughout the history of the medium. He insisted that only one example of his own work be included, a Second World War photograph of a shattered building at Tobruk in the Western Desert (70). It was while we were working together that he visited the Imperial War Museum to choose a selection of his war photographs for the retrospective exhibition sponsored by Kodak in honour of his seventieth birthday. For him these war pictures were the high point of the exhibition. He asked me to write the introduction to it and I recall how moved I was by those strange and unfamiliar images. Between then and his death in January 1980 he sometimes considered ways of using his Ministry of Information photographs and in December 1979, when invited by the Imperial War Museum to collaborate in the production of a book and a major exhibition, he agreed enthusiastically and thought the suggestion an 'inspiration'. Sadly, Sir Cecil was never able to see the project through.

I feel honoured and happy that I was asked to select the photographs and write the text for this book. It is one of my greatest pleasures to have known him as a friend, while as a colleague he taught me much about seeing, style and art.

The picture selection was guided by several criteria. The key to a successful art book is winnowing pictures until only masterworks are left. But this book does not try merely to reconfirm Beaton as an artist with a camera. It is a survey of his photographs for the Ministry of Information, from army manoeuvres to portraits of the Shah of Persia. They show he was able to fulfil commonplace assignments, such as recording a day in the life of a pilot, and that he was excellent at making propaganda pictures, such as those of children in hospitals.

Beaton could photograph well only if he saw beauty through the lens. Looking at these pictures one is aware of how much beauty he saw in places or faces where others would see none. As a war photographer it was not just out of fear, which was strong enough, that he chose not to go near the front; carnage and death he could not record. It was not the human drama but the spirit that interested him. And the form. Style, that ingredient which spiced all his other work, had little place here.

Beaton saw that the true weapon of war was strength of character. Eyes of soldiers and civilians told him more about how the war would be won than row after row of tanks. The war would be won, according to Beaton's vision, because 'These warriors, factory workers and civilians alike, who took courage and heroism for granted, were so imbued with the general spirit of the time, that they could not be deflected from their sense of duty and were possessed of a morale that was untouched by the loss of worldly possessions or by physical discomfort.'[2] Human life was too amazing and too precious to be destroyed by the forces of evil. This is at the heart of his wartime photography.

Beaton was conditioned from his earliest days as a cameraman to flatter. His writing was often stinging but his portraits were generous. One wonders, however, had he photographed Hitler or Stalin, whom he described as 'two of the world's most loathsome monsters', what the pictures would have been like.

Had Cecil Beaton written this book, it would look and read quite differently, but the actual picture selection might have been similar. For *The Magic Image* we studied thousands of photographs together and discussed their merits, and we came to know each other's taste. I am familiar with his ideas about design but it would have been wrong to try to imitate them here. Rather, I have sought to retain the integrity of each picture by presenting it as Cecil Beaton saw the scene at the time of exposure. The full-frame of his 2¼ inch square negatives has a wholeness that is quite balanced and best left alone. The picture sections are arranged chronologically but the sequence of the photographs within them is not.

During the war the Ministry of Information was responsible for maintaining public morale. When in 1940 Cecil Beaton was asked to undertake official commissions the MOI was particularly anxious to increase the supply of photographs available for distribution to the press. Beaton was chosen because he was the best known English photographer – 'world's greatest photographer' and 'most celebrated photographer' proclaimed the British press – and because of his social connections. The photographs he took for the Ministry of the services, bomb damage, the civilian war effort, hospitals, factories, the campaign in North Africa, the fighting in Burma and scenes in India and China were widely reproduced during the war in many newspapers, magazines, books and travelling exhibitions.

For Beaton the commission from the MOI in 1940 was a blessing. He sincerely wanted to serve his country and photography was something he knew he could do well. Although other photographers were commissioned by the Ministry Beaton enjoyed special privileges and opportunities. The resulting photographs form a unique and diversified collection.

Brief Biography

Cecil Beaton was born in London on 14 January 1904, the eldest of four children. The family was upper middle class, his father being a successful timber merchant. When very young he showed a strong interest in the theatre, painting, photography and fashionable society and these predominated over more academic pursuits during his school years at Harrow and later as an undergraduate at Cambridge. They remained the preoccupations of his adult life, with the addition of writing, travelling and gardening. He always had to work for a living and his income was derived mostly from fashion and portrait photography and designing for the theatre and cinema.

Beaton's first public recognition came in the 1920s. Influenced by the theatre photographs of E O Hoppé and the fashion pictures of Baron de Meyer, he soon developed his own style of incorporating his sitters into ever more complicated and ornate back-drops and settings. He wanted the people he posed in front of the camera to look like actors and actresses. The personality or character of the person was incidental to the overall design and feeling of the composition.

His first exhibition in 1929 established his reputation as an extremely clever young photographer. That same year he left for America, literally to seek his fortune. Arriving in New York, Beaton began at once photographing the very rich and soon added celebrities to his customers when Condé Nast acknowledged that the young Englishman's work was good enough for *Vogue*. Before leaving America Beaton signed a contract with Nast which assured him an annual income and work when he returned the following year. He had to put away his amateurish No. 3A folding pocket Kodak (he had been using it since his teens) and buy an 8 × 10 inch studio camera for the shots of fashion models and Hollywood stars which became his bread and butter in the 1930s. He also made excellent portraits of Salvador Dali, Orson Wells, Aldous Huxley, Jean Cocteau, W H Auden and Picasso. These show a mature and powerful style of portraiture with just a few props specifically suited to the sitter. His fame increased in 1937 when he was the only photographer invited to take photographs immediately before the wedding of the former King Edward VIII and Mrs Wallis Simpson. But he jeopardised his reputation by incorporating anti-Jewish remarks in a sketch he did for *Vogue* published in 1938. This attitude, which he later greatly regretted, was common enough in high society at that time but resulted in much press attention and a forced resignation from *Vogue*.

Though rarely discussed, the travel photographs which Beaton took before 1940 are extremely important in the context of his war work. Because Beaton is known for using carefully constructed sets and back-drops, one often overlooks his candid pictures of the streets of New York, Dubrovnik and Algiers. Capturing people with split-second exposures in natural attitudes and on the move was a revolutionary advance in photography in the 1930s, made possible by the introduction of the Ermanox, Leica and Rolleiflex cameras and new types of film. Beaton was one of the pioneers of these techniques and experimented with them in Haiti, Tangiers, Greece, Mexico, Russia, Tunisia, Venice, Rome, Switzerland, Turkey and around the Mediterranean. In 1938 he published some fascinating documentary work in *Cecil Beaton's New York*. In *Time Exposure*, a selection of his photographs with commentary by Peter Quennell published in 1941, Beaton showed that although he was not an exceptional photo-journalist, he had a keen interest in the patterns of overhead tram-lines, Greek architecture, rooftops in North Africa and native people of different cultures selling their wares in crowded alleys. His experience of reacting as a photographer to the real world of constantly changing shapes and moods and subjects was vitally important for the work he would be asked to do during the war.

His skill at stylised portraiture also prepared him for his wartime commissions. Most notable was his fairytale depiction of Queen Elizabeth in 1939. She is seen at Buckingham Palace in evening dress and jewels, looking serene and invincible. Indeed, such a Queen was worth fighting for, a dream queen who embodied beauty and centuries of British monarchy. Released just after the outbreak of the war, these photographs were enthusiastically taken up by *The Times*, *Manchester Guardian*, *Daily Mirror*, *Queen*, *Evening News*, *Daily Sketch*, *Harper's Bazaar*, *The Tatler*, *Daily Telegraph*, *Daily Mail* and other newspapers and magazines. All linked these visions of the Queen with the name Cecil Beaton. And they often stated categorically that these were the best pictures ever taken of her.

During the war Beaton continued, intermittently, to take fashion photographs for British *Vogue*, portraits for *The Sketch*, and costume and set designs for Hollywood films and the London theatre, and he also photographed successful stage productions. His fashion pictures were sometimes set against bomb-damaged buildings or a row of modest terraced houses. The style originated before the war when Beaton placed elegant models reading newspapers amongst débris in what seemed like shattered rooms. This disturbing vision shocked editors. After the war he continued with this more 'realistic' style and he declared the pre-war fashions and photographs 'obsolete'. He wrote in *The Best of Beaton* that 'The posed, static hands with the pointed index finger and arched wrist acquired an overnight vulgarity; the celestial expression in the eyes suddenly became a joke shared by everyone except the sitter. The earlier pictures appeared over re-touched and altogether too artificial, with ladies with forced rosebud simpers and impossible golden curls.'[3] It was not just Beaton who had changed; the whole world had.

The years from 1944 to 1948 were 'Happy Years', as his diaries for this period are called – celebrating liberation day in Paris, acting in *Lady Windermere's Fan*, working in New York with a self-confidence hitherto lacking, having a love affair with Greta Garbo, and designing costumes and sets for Sir Alexander Korda's films and Frederick Ashton's ballets. He searched for and found his perfect country retreat – Reddish House in Broadchalke, Wiltshire.

An obscure but fascinating book which Cecil Beaton published in 1944 is entitled *British Photographers*. Decades before the current general enthusiasm for old photographs, he praised the pictures of then unknown photographers such as David Octavius Hill and Julia Margaret Cameron, who today are considered masters of the medium. His fascination with the history of photography culminated in *The Magic Image*: *The Genius of Photography from 1839 to the Present Day*, published in 1975. Knowledge of how men and women have used the camera and his deep love of painting enhanced his own work greatly.

His books from the forties and fifties include: *History Under Fire* with James Pope-Hennessy, *Air of Glory*, *Winged Squadrons*, *Near East*, *Far East*, *India*, *An Indian Album*, *Chinese Album*, *Photobiography*, *Persona Grata* with Kenneth Tynan and *The Glass of Fashion*. His play *The Gainsborough Girls* was performed at the Theatre Royal in Brighton in 1951; he was made a CBE in 1957 and fifteen years later was knighted. In 1965 he was awarded two Oscars for the décor and costumes of the film *My Fair Lady*. Cecil Beaton led too active a life for a quick summary of it all. Throughout his career he befriended and photographed the most eminent and colourful people of each decade. He had exhibitions of his paintings, stage designs and photographs. He served as a Royal photographer. He won Academy Awards. He published thirty books including six volumes of diaries. After a severe stroke in 1974 he continued to paint and write, and in 1979, the year before he died, he photographed the Paris fashion shows for French *Vogue*. He had more style than almost anyone. He dressed magnificently and lived with great panache. He could be impossible and he could be very kind. He surrounded himself with beautiful things and witty, intelligent, creative or famous people. He was perceptive and talented in extraordinary ways.

The War Begins

'This war, as far as I can see, is something specifically designed to show up my inadequacy in every possible capacity,' complained Cecil Beaton soon after Britain declared war on Germany. 'I am too incompetent to enlist as a private in the army. It's doubtful if I'd be much good at camouflage – in any case my repeated requests to join have been met with "You'll be called if you're wanted." '[4] Beaton's sentiments could not have been more egocentric. He was depressed because he did not know what to do with himself, especially as the desire to help assure victory for his country ran deep.

Since 1930 Beaton had leased a charming old country house in Wiltshire called Ashcombe. Whenever he was not working in London, New York or Hollywood, he rested, wrote, gardened and entertained there. It was his first home of his own. In September 1939 he volunteered for part-time duty with his local civil defence organisation. He became a night telephonist at the air raid precautions centre at Wilton, not far from Ashcombe. He drank tea through the night with an odd assortment of companions and prayed that he would not get either himself or the telephone wires in a muddle. The work was not difficult but tedious, and for Beaton tedium was a torment to be avoided at all times.

He had an idea, typically Beatonesque, to produce a play to entertain the troops training on nearby Salisbury Plain. Costumes, décor, music, witty words – certainly the creation of a pantomime was a better way of using his talents than sitting by telephones. It was not until the war was well under way that he stopped seeing life as theatre and fabrication more stimulating than reality.

With John Sutro he wrote the script for *Heil Cinderella* and enlisted friends such as Edith Oliver (Mayor of Wilton), Lady Juliet Duff and Donald Masters, to play the various roles. Beaton was an Ugly Sister. He scurried about getting fabrics for his costume designs and organising his rather aristocratic but unprofessional cast. When the play opened in December 1939 many newspapers ran photographs of him dressed for his role. He was a celebrity, the first photographer in English history who regularly made news. The company, suffering from sore throats and runny noses, played to servicemen in Wiltshire and took the show to London and Brighton to raise money for the 'Cigarettes for the Troops' fund. This extravaganza lasted four months.

At the beginning of the war the Ministry of Information already had a Photographs Section, which formed part of the General Production Division. A memorandum in January 1940 summarised the existing situation regarding official photography. Official army photographs were criticised for being 'Too static. Lack of massed power – Taken with eye to British popular Press. Very few "angle" shots are available.'[5] The Ministry was better pleased with the work being done by, for example, the two official Royal Air Force photographers but the nine-page document left no doubt that the government was greatly concerned about the nature of the visual records being produced and circulated at home and abroad.

Soon afterwards Beaton was asked to accept official commissions from the Ministry of Information. In *The Best of Beaton* he wrote:

> When war was declared I knew myself to be incapable of filling any regular service job. Fortunately, Hugh Francis in the M. of I., at the suggestion of Sir Kenneth Clark, saw fit to employ me as a photographer. At first the assignments were somewhat tentative: was this really the person to give us posters to prevent loss of life by careless talk, or to encourage recruiting into the services? The novice tried his hand at reportage: munitions factories and training schools, barrage-balloon maintenance, the guns pointing out to sea on the chalk Dover cliffs, and the arrival in the country, from urban areas, of snotty-nosed children, with tickets pinned to their backs. Then portraits of war leaders in their Whitehall offices . . .[6]

As Controller of the Home Publicity Division and Chairman of the War Artists Advisory Committee, Kenneth Clark, the Director of the National Gallery in London, played a major part in obtaining commissions for suitable artists to record the war effort.

Beaton was delighted to have a definite role. The Ministry thought it was quite a coup to have him undertaking assignments for them. No matter how the pictures turned out, they would carry the name 'Cecil Beaton' and be interesting to the viewer for at least two reasons – the subject portrayed and the fact that this was the way Beaton saw it. What Cecil Beaton saw and did and the people he associated with were of interest to all strata of British society. If he could help keep up morale then he was performing a vital service to the nation. After the war his lavishly

illustrated books and articles about his experiences still commanded a large
readership.

Some of his first assignments were to visit shipyards and munitions and aircraft
factories. The results were prosaic although they were no doubt useful to the
Ministry in its pamphlets and exhibitions and as material to distribute to the press.
It would be wrong, however, to suggest that the MOI was always satisfied with the
standard of Beaton's work and there were some clashes over the special
arrangements he demanded. This first group of photographs lacked drama and an
original viewpoint. They do not convey the crouching, the measuring, the sweat,
that is all part of a labouring job. Beaton was too detached from his subjects and
there is none of the spiritual bond between the artist and the workers that one feels
in Henry Moore's drawings of coal miners or Stanley Spencer's paintings of
shipbuilders, also done for the MOI.

Coincidentally, it was on this theme of production that three years later Beaton
was asked to write the introduction to the second volume of the second series of a
popular set of small books originated by the MOI entitled *War Pictures by British
Artists*. These artists were under the official direction of Kenneth Clark's
committee. Beaton's introduction gives a clue as to why some of the initial
assignments in 1940 for the Ministry were not so successful:

> After three years of war, the Minister of Production announces, 'We are making the
> right kind of tanks now.' Perhaps it is also permissible to say of our war artists that they
> are painting the right kind of pictures now. Artists are considered to be more sensitive,
> more emotional beings than Cabinet Ministers; and though some of them had for a long
> time past seen the inevitability of this war, when the war came a number of these
> painters, writers and poets suffered such an overwhelming shock that as artists they
> became sterile. In order to justify their existence, some joined the ranks of the Services;
> others felt that they must employ their talents more suitably, yet still were incapable of
> finding the right approach to their means of expression.
> . . . after three years the artists have accepted the grim seriousness of a war which has
> to be fought out with no short cuts to victory. 'Tears, toil, grit, guts, blood, steel and
> sweat' are, in fact, its key words.
> Most of the war pictures, to-day, try to convey the emotional impact of this desperate
> and grave history. Perhaps a small percentage of artists are making painstaking records
> that could be as effectively and accurately made by the press photographers; but here,
> with the subject of 'Production', we are fortunate that much of the material – mines,
> foundries, workshops – is for technical reasons beyond the power of the camera to
> reproduce, or at any rate to reproduce in its full significance. In those vulcan forges of
> the armament workshops and aircraft production factories, our eyes become attuned,
> unlike the camera lens, to the nuances of darkness amid a strange world that is
> spasmodically suffused by flashes of green, magenta, puce and golden light. In this
> world of molten metals, of glowing furnaces, soot and firework sparks, that only the
> painter can interpret, Graham Sutherland has reverently seized his opportunity to
> capture this fleeting phenomenon of sequined brilliance, of mystery, of glowing magic
> . . . Henry Moore's troglodytes, crouching with a little more than the muscles of their
> insect-like bodies and their eye of electric light visible in the gloom of the coal mines,
> could be expressed in no other medium.[7]

Beaton's war pictures never sustained the kind of intensity of vision and execution
that he describes above. He did at times produce evocative, mystical, dynamic
images but it was rare that any series had, for example, the haunting grandeur of
Henry Moore's drawings or Bill Brandt's photographs of London underground
shelters. Part of the reason was that, as he often admitted, he had difficulty in
concentrating.

Frequently he solved photo-journalistic problems in the most expeditious manner and he knew he was not always creating works of art. The passage quoted shows how well he knew the difference. But sometimes he became so receptive to the surroundings, so fired with a vision of the meaning of the human condition, of civilisation being destroyed, that his pictures resound with truth and beauty. What he said of other artists, that they were 'incapable of finding the right approach to their means of expression', was partly true of Beaton himself. But his commission was not simply a licence to express himself. He was given assignments that had to be carried out in a set period and if he was not always particularly original he nevertheless always did his job. He found comfort in that he usually could, as he wrote, 'find groups and settings that would compose into a design'.

Portraits of war leaders were used repeatedly in the daily press and in magazines. They had to be presented as strong, intelligent and humane. Their faces must not become monotonous; they must always appear at the very least interesting and as often as possible remarkable personages. This is an area in which Beaton excelled, except when he allowed the trappings of refinement to become too intrusive. Ernest Bevin while posing on the grand staircase of the Ministry of Labour told Beaton, 'You're trying to make me look more Royalist than the King! I suppose you think America expects me to have the Duke of Buccleuch's background.' If all the portraits Beaton made during the war, especially in India, were hung together, one would imagine a world peopled with kings, queens and princes. But he could also take portraits that were powerful and direct, such as the famous one of Churchill sitting at his desk showing fierce determination (49). Beaton had only ten minutes with the Prime Minister and the picture is the result of two strong-willed men each determined to have what he wanted – Churchill to get rid of the photographer, Beaton to obtain the definitive portrait.

Beaton had made many portraits of cabinet ministers, generals and admirals before he left for America in May 1940. The Churchill picture, which was to become one of the best-known images of the war, was taken soon after his return in September. (He had gone to America to earn money from fashion assignments but felt guilt-ridden and was relieved to return home.) When it was released on 23 December 1940 the Glasgow newspaper the *Daily Record and Mail* captioned the Churchill picture: 'Hitler? Send him in! Did someone mention Hitler and his Nazis? All the Premier's determination to rid the world of the canker that threatens it is revealed in this latest portrait, by Cecil Beaton, of Britain's chosen leader.' The *Illustrated London News* issued the picture as a special photogravure supplement with the comment: 'This forceful portrait is suitable for framing.' And thousands did frame it. This snapshot taken with a Rolleiflex was hung in homes, offices and pubs; reproduced in newspapers, magazines and calendars; and made into posters and postcards.

Another success in portraiture at this time was the series of pictures of Eileen Dunne, a three-year-old bomb victim sitting wide-eyed in her hospital bed. Though often criticised for being too sentimental and contrived, the photographs are masterly (13). This solitary little girl with her big questioning eyes and her bandaged head, who appeared on the cover of *Life* magazine and in the *Illustrated London News* in September 1940, became a symbol of the terrifying destruction launched by Germany on the people of Great Britain. The picture aroused much sympathy in America for the British cause.

The Blitz left Wren churches, East End buildings, the Houses of Parliament, South Kensington museums and much more partly or completely destroyed. Photographing the ruins turned Beaton into a war artist. Not until then did he find a style of his own that could effectively evoke the war. Whether in the smoking débris or in the empty corridors of Buckingham Palace he discovered shapes and forms that spoke poetically of a world coming apart. His images of the burning and crumbling city were balanced by scenes of farming, which he was able to imbue with the same intensity. Sometimes his pictures were surrealistic, as when a bomb in Piccadilly blew out store windows and mannequins were propelled into the street, or when he photographed a wax head on a pile of rubble and incidentally infuriated passers-by by focusing on such a gruesome object. But the best pictures were the ones that allowed the disparate shapes to dominate and speak in the powerful language of abstraction.

During the Blitz, James Pope-Hennessy and Cecil Beaton collaborated on the book *History Under Fire*. It was divided into three sections – The Attack on Medieval and Renaissance London, The Attack on Wren's London and The Attack on Hanoverian London – and explained what these newly destroyed buildings represented in the past. In the early morning, after a raid, Pope-Hennessy and Beaton would go to the site of a once noble edifice, one to reflect and the other to photograph. In the preface to the book, Pope-Hennessy wrote:

> . . . in so far as it is possible to convey the early horror of the ruins, and also their melancholy appearance, Mr Beaton's photographs do this. In taking them he has earned the gratitude not merely of contemporaries anxious to assess the damage to London history, but of posterity; for surely his series of ruined churches, streets and houses may prove as documentarily important as Hollar's engravings of the area devastated by the Great Fire of London in 1666. The merits these photographs display in other ways – composition, grandeur, tragedy, the strange vitality of wreckage – are too unusual and too evident to require indication.[8]

Beaton not only photographed bomb-damaged buildings and casualties but made gentle and touching pictures of evacuated children (3). He sometimes wandered into basement shelters or the underground at night, but these photographs lack the mystery and drama that the 'subterranean' bodies evoked in other artists.

Specifically military assignments in 1940 included work with the army and navy. Beaton spent some time in the summer photographing army training on Salisbury Plain (41–42). These pictures often suggest boys playing with toys rather than men on serious military exercises. At the end of the year *Vogue*, the *Illustrated London News* and *The Sketch* carried Cecil Beaton's feature stories on the Women's Royal Naval Service. These women seemed forever marching from one building to the next or posing against neo-classical columns or mimicking figureheads (35). However, the picture of six Wren stewards in the Painted Hall at the Royal Naval College, Greenwich (36), is haunting. The women appear phantom-like in a centuries-old setting, silent, monastic, the antithesis of war.

Pics of RAF

Propaganda

In about March 1941 Beaton received a commission from Hugh Francis, Director of the Photographs Division of the M O I, that would involve him in many months of work. It was to make a documentary record of the Royal Air Force. At this stage of the war the Royal Air Force offered the only means of striking directly at Germany. Beaton had already made some brief visits to R A F stations and knew at first-hand about their life and death struggle during the Battle of Britain the previous year. They were the heroes of the war and the public wanted to know where they came from, how they were trained, how they lived and how they died. Beaton photographed the recruitment and training of airmen, and the three principal types of R A F station – Bomber Command, Fighter Command and Coastal Command – as well as the Women's Auxiliary Air Force. He described his feelings about this work in his war diary, *The Years Between*:

> Looking at a batch of photographs I had taken – the result of cursory visits to various R A F stations – Hugh Francis of the Ministry of Information said, 'It's rather surprising that you enjoy doing this – they're so different from the stuff you used to publish.' But although my subject matter had changed so violently, often my approach with the camera was the same in that, wherever I went, I was trying to find groups and settings that would compose into a design. Often the bare walls or the struts of a hangar lent themselves as usefully to a pictorial scheme as any more calculated effects of decoration.
>
> The fact that here were people of character living under dramatic conditions inspired me to adopt a more realistic approach, and the freedom of doing a straightforward piece of reportage was something that I found stimulating. My equipment consisted of one Rolleiflex and a flashbulb, so my powers of ingenuity were given full rein.
>
> Hugh Francis told me he would authorise my making a complete study of the R A F. Apart from the uses he would make of the photographs, I should write a fictional composition, written for propaganda. At last, I felt, I was able to do something to assuage my pangs of guilt at being unable to make a more worthwhile contribution.[9]

The book that resulted – *Winged Squadrons* – is one of Beaton's most tenderly written and the photographs are some of his most sincere.

> One is astonished at the youthfulness of these seventeen-year olds with their subtle English looks, clear complexions, and thatch of hair shorn closely over the ears. One bright young man asked when my picture would appear, and in answer to my 'in six weeks' time' said, 'Oh, most of us will be dead by then!'[10]

He added that 'most of the R A F volunteers are utterly fulfilled in their job . . . They are neither pining for home, lusting after girls, nor fretting about danger. It is all much happier and simpler than I'd imagined.' He dedicated *Winged Squadrons* 'To the Parents Who Have Given Their Sons to the Royal Air Force'.

The book was a combination of propaganda and rhetoric. It proves Beaton to be a fine propagandist, but his diaries confirm that many of the sentiments were his own. The writing and the pictures show a loss of self-consciousness which is atypical. In his other books Beaton is the central character: what he sees and how he responds is the theme. But in *Winged Squadrons* he is discussing and illustrating valour, patriotism and other human attributes that struck him as something wonderful and deserving of as much praise as he could give. He wrote:

> . . . Never before in history has our country been saved by so youthful a fraternity fighting with such casual perfection. The lads have acquired a sense of responsibility which has given them the maturity of older men.

A new mould of men has been cast. The feats of their bravery haunt us, they baffle us, and satisfy completely the spirit of romantic daring inherent in our island race. Perhaps this British aptitude for flying is part of the sailing tradition and the feeling for freedom and adventure that is a heritage from Drake.[11]

The photographs of the men were taken from many angles with a conscious attempt to present an intimate picture. We see the recruits having their medical examinations looking up past a syringe to a bare light-bulb (15). In another photograph it is as though we were standing just behind a new arrival being kitted out, a streak of light between him and the men who are part of the world he is about to enter (14). He must cross that streak of light both physically and spiritually to become one of them and the photograph is a magnificent symbolic image representing the transformation. A picture of R A F recruits marching past a sphinx is both comical but again, also symbolic (17). These men, like the sphinx, must be part animal, part human. They must fight for survival and protect their territory. They must be cunning and instinctive while they apply their brain power to the handling of sophisticated aircraft and machinery. The photograph of two young airmen (18) with their books, one looking out into space, the other studying, combines in a single image the two sides of training – the acquisition of knowledge and the time to prepare emotionally for possible death.

Beaton's pilots relaxing and waiting have the quality of individual movie frames. There seems to be a long story leading up to that moment and a long one to follow (19–20). Only the smiling fighter pilot in front of his Hurricane is complete (23). Photographs 25 to 30 are part of a feature on Bomber Command. Hugh Francis had suggested to Cecil Beaton that he document a bomber pilot's day, and a handsome young officer was selected. His name was fictionalised in *Winged Squadrons* as Robert Tring.

Only nineteen years old, he had brought back his crew and aircraft, B for Bobby, from twenty-nine bombing trips over Berlin. To see him quietly reading in his room you would never suspect that he had enough strength of muscle to take up and bring down a heavy Stirling bomber. Yet he is considered one of the most steady and reliable pilots of the squadron. The son of a clergyman, aesthetic-looking, with strong, rather feminine features, lean, with the long well-formed hands of a violinist, and the dark quiet voice of a scholar, he is the perfect contrast to the type our enemy produces, and represents the nobility of our cause. From the way Bobby chain-smokes, and casts a slightly haunted look out of the corner of his eyes, it might be concluded that he is showing the first signs of fatigue. But one trip more and Bobby will be leaving his station, for though he wishes to be sent 'out East,' he will soon be posted to a training school to become a flying instructor.[12]

The pictures of Bobby have a sensual quality; he is for Beaton a romantic hero.

Air of Glory

Air of Glory is the title of Beaton's finest wartime book and, except for a short introduction and captions, it consists entirely of photographs. It was issued by the Ministry of Information late in 1941 and includes the full range of subjects he had taken. The magnificence of the book is not solely in its individual pictures but in the vigour of its presentation. Much of this is due to the skill of the unnamed designer, who appears to have been Bauhaus-trained. The strong photographs, the typography, the ever-changing picture spreads, the excellent reproductions,

Beaton's lyrical foreword and even the flowery captions written by the novelist Rosamond Lehmann all combine to make an inspiring publication.

In the preface to *Air of Glory* Cecil Beaton wrote:

> I wanted to show the various groups as vignettes, isolated as I saw them from one another, occupied at their separate units; the hermits at their remote searchlight or gun post, scattered from the white cliffs of Dover to the Shetland Islands; the invigorating sight of the workers, coolly efficient in spite of acrid air and the hubbub of noise in the Vulcan's Forge heat of the aircraft production factory, as well as the self-deprecating heroes of the air and the men aboard the mine-sweepers and corvettes. It was my intention to show some of the homelier scenes as well, the Cockney children transplanted into the nursery school among the green Downs, the spinster lady wrapping packages or filing card indexes for the Prisoners of War, the housewife, perhaps rather lonely, but fighting valiantly on the home front, and the inevitable scenes at the crowded railway junctions, and in every canteen, with its tea urns, buns, lanyards, and perhaps its packets of cigarettes.[13]

Beaton succeeds in creating a montage of activity, of individuals participating in a great cause.

Preparing books for publication was not part of the usual brief for official wartime photographers. To the Ministry Beaton was a celebrity who could write, design and photograph; he could produce the kind of books people wanted to buy. In turn, Beaton was infuriated when his work was not used.

Air of Glory helped Beaton to consolidate his unique position. He wrote: 'I have been fortunate, more than fortunate, in being able to see in a way less lucky, more stationary workers are denied, how the varying strata of humanity are rallying to the country's call. My camera has provided me with magic passes on to the sea and into the air.'[14] Beaton states in the preface that 'The resilience of the people and the unconsciousness of the fact that they are brave . . . cannot be photographed except on the mind.' He felt his limitations as a photographer even more acutely now that his senses were attuned, like those of all his compatriots, to the bombs and the silences, the destruction and the new buds of spring. 'The horrors of what is at stake quickened our awareness of England's beauty,' he wrote. 'Never before have we loved it more.'

The Middle East

> Now that my RAF book [*Winged Squadrons*] has been sent to the printers [February 1942] I am looking around for my next job. My ambition is to be sent to the Near East. Randolph Churchill, on leave, was enthusiastic and helpful. I go to see Brendan Bracken on Wednesday, and there is a chance that the Ministry of Information may send me to Cairo to take photographs and do articles for another book. It is a thrilling prospect, and there is now a star shining brightly in front of me.[15]

Beaton was given twenty-four hours' notice to collect the necessary passes, certificates, equipment and luggage and to arrive at Euston Station for the start of his Middle Eastern adventure. He had no time to read his instructions until he was seated on the train to Scotland:

> Accuracy is what we must have in your reports; bring back as much information as possible, but we must be able to check and counter-check for accuracy. Your reports to be written in a free colloquial style. Photographs: A case of three hundred flash bulbs will be on the boat. These you must look after; the films have already gone ahead to Cairo.[16]

During the next four months that film would wind through his Rolleiflex as he travelled from Cairo to the Western Desert and on to Tehran, Baghdad, Jerusalem, Amman, Beirut and Lisbon. But now on a cold February morning in Glasgow in 1942 he waited for his ship, HMS *Alcantara*, a former luxury liner converted into a troopship, part of a convoy bound for Freetown, Sierra Leone. As he travelled comfortably to warmer waters he sketched and photographed the sailors and airmen on board (57–59).

> The Ministry of Information had asked me to take photographs for them of the west coast of Africa. I had been supplied with letters pointing out that if necessary the films should be handed over to the authorities for development and, that if the pictures could not be published, they would be useful for records, or secret files: 'Yes, yes,' said the official, 'I quite understand, everything's in order, but you see you've got a camera and my instructions here are to let no one pass with a camera.'[17]

Not only could he not photograph in Sierra Leone, but he was transferred to the *Altmark II*, a notoriously dirty, 3,000-ton ship with 'an alarming list'. Of the move he wrote: 'We arrived into the dark, black, greasy bowels of this small ship.' Worse, however, was the waiting. No one seemed to know how long this nightmarish confinement would last before they got permission to sail. Eventually, as in a dream, he was called off the ship and flown to Cairo, the headquarters of Middle East Command.

For his forthcoming tour of the Western Desert he had been lent by the MOI to the Air Ministry. The first problem he faced upon arriving in Cairo was what to wear:

> In London the Ministry of Information were baffled as to whether I, being 'a special case', should wear a uniform or not: if so, to which Service was I to be attached? Would I be a private or a non-commissioned officer? 'Best to leave it till your arrival in Cairo. They'll know what to make of you.' But HQ were equally baffled. 'He can't go into the desert without a uniform. Someone, sooner or later, would be bound to shoot him for a spy.' 'We can't possibly make him an officer,' said a grey-haired group-captain, scratching his head. I was rather sad to hear this, as ever since my childhood I have suspected I would never get beyond being a private. In the end it was arranged that I should wear RAF uniform with 'Official Photographer' on the shoulders instead of a badge of rank . . . I have now learnt that I was supplied with a heterogeneous collection of garments that would ordinarily have belonged either to a high-ranking officer, or to someone in the ranks, but not to both at the same time.[18]

After only one week in Cairo he was sent to the desert, having been told:

> 'We want "might" in our propaganda here. Don't photograph one aeroplane, photograph sixty at a time – never take four tanks, but a hundred! Get them to "lay on" some important demonstration! Ask for the impossible!'[19]

But later he would write:

> I came to the desert thinking I was nearer to war; yet even here war seems distant.
> Where then is war? In Whitehall . . . it necessarily seems remote. Here I see how much spade work goes on continuously behind the lines . . . I see how many hours of dreary waiting and inconvenience must be endured each day, or how much time can be spent repairing an accumulator or a lorry, bringing in trays of tea, or doing chores . . . I see that human existence in the desert has not the proportion of the surroundings. Yet I realize that all these aspects are as real a part of war as another.[20]

It is difficult at times to see Cecil Beaton's work as 'war photographs'. We identify war with the shooting of guns, the dropping of bombs, front-line action, the dead. In other words acts of destruction, not the routine of daily life. But almost the entire body of Beaton's work excludes the former; his eye was focused on the small details behind the battlefield. Beaton's photographs of sailors sewing or asleep, camels pulling heavy rollers to prepare a desert runway, R A F airmen waiting for transport or drinking in the camp bar, facing a dust-storm, typing letters and sitting behind a desk are as much images of war as the more violent ones.

The most dramatic scenes for Beaton in the desert war were the burnt-out tanks and aircraft looking like skeletons of strange mechanical monsters. One cannot help but compare these new ruins with other desert monuments – the Sphinx, the pyramids, the palaces of Karnak and ask: what do we mean by the progress of civilisation?

> During my long professional career no problems ever perplexed me more than those I encountered when trying to take pictures of the Eighth Army. Apart from difficulties of light and atmosphere, there was the problem of sand which crept into the camera, often causing a shutter to misfire or a series of black stripes to appear on my negative, so that every evening I had to spend much time in a hermetically sealed tent, meticulously flicking every cranny of my equipment with a water-colour paintbrush. These were additional difficulties of which I was not aware until the photographic results came through and I saw how banal was the effect of many of my negatives. If, as usually happened, the sun was high and the sky innocent of cloud, my subject – whether wrecked building, tents, or machines – would be suffused with a deadening, though brilliant light, which caused it to disappear into the background haze. Try to photograph the faces of men in the desert in most daytime conditions and they will appear black and with the crowns of their heads and the tips of their noses vividly illuminated. Photographing in a sandstorm is like photographing in a November fog. Only after dawn and just before sunset does the light provide a third dimension.[21]

For this reason Beaton took photographs such as (64) from underneath the fuselage of an aircraft. He was desperate to find interesting lighting and here, there were shadows creating a strong pattern with the emerging legs of a faceless man. He also found that photographs taken within an arm's length often produced better effects than long-distance ones: 'Pictures of discharged cartridge cases, gas marks, and empty tins lying at one's feet create the most vivid impressions of modern warfare.'

> The Surrealists have anticipated this battle ground. In all their paintings, now proved to be prophetic, we have seen the eternal incongruities. The carcases of burnt-out aeroplanes lying in the middle of a vast panorama: overturned trucks: deserted lorries: cars that have been buckled by machine-gun fire, with their under parts pouring out in grotesque, tortured shapes: some unaccountable clothing blown into the telephone wires, or drapery in a tree: the shattered walls: the sunsets of bright unforgettable colours. All these have been faithfully reproduced by Dali, Max Ernst, Joan Miro, long before the war.[22]

The unremitting sun beating down on Beaton led him to see not only in surrealistic terms but also in abstract ones.

The picture of the shell-shattered fire station in Tobruk (70) is one of the finest of his career. Abstract, with almost every detail on one plane, the differently shaped pieces of the ceiling seem to be floating without any purpose or direction. Looking closer one sees that they are connected by wires in a delicate balance. The picture might be a metaphor for the war: the world is being shattered into many pieces;

both the large and the small are holding on tenuously; what survives and what falls is largely a matter of chance.

Such symbolic visions of the war did not dominate Beaton's Middle Eastern photography. Both in Cairo and in the field he was required to photograph civilian and military leaders as well as ordinary soldiers. Much of his time was spent writing the detailed captions explaining who these men were and what they were doing. The pictures of Air Chief Marshal Sir Arthur Tedder, Air Vice-Marshal Sir Arthur Coningham and Sir Miles and Lady Lampson were extremely useful for Ministry purposes and are included here because of their important roles in the Middle East. Only the portrait of Colonel Philip Astley, an army public relations officer, is completely successful in an artistic sense, the lighting effectively setting him off, icon-like, against his surroundings (81). The background has many rectangular shapes forming crosses and the picture of King George VI is hung so that it touches the rim of a large woven crown. This military man and his office appear more ecclesiastical than secular.

Beaton's favourite desert subject was the Long Range Desert Group, which he saw as having mythological attributes.

> . . . A more grotesquely assorted, more frightening-looking bunch of bandits it would be hard to imagine. Bearded, covered with dust, with blood-shot eyes, they were less of the world of today than like primeval warriors, or timeless inhabitants of a remote hemisphere . . .
> Stirling and the Long Range Desert Group, the highwaymen of the desert, have made a legend for themselves with their extremely scientific, yet romantic, pirate-story adventures. Sometimes for months on end they patrol the desert ocean in armoured vehicles equipped with radios. Often they penetrate miles behind the enemy's lines, take him by surprise at night, burn army lorries, destroy tanks, and blow up vital equipment. This war is one of machines and technical efficiency: it allows little scope for individual escapades by groups of men. But the very specialized warfare that the Long Range Desert Group have perfected is an exception. It is one which the Germans, thus far, have ignored or have not dared to undertake.[23]

But he did not know quite how to photograph them, and the pictures are rather too naturalistic, for example when they are smoking or reading letters from home, or too orchestrated, as in (72) which shows them walking through an archway.

Beaton spent three months photographing and writing in Cairo and the desert. In June 1942 he began his tour of the countries of the Middle East which were friendly to Britain. He went to Tehran to record the Persians and British working on various joint industrial projects and to photograph the Shah. Upon seeing him and his stunning first wife Queen Fawzieh, sister of King Farouk of Egypt, he was immediately transformed back into a Hollywood glamour photographer. They looked young, beautiful, rich and modern as they sat by the side of their swimming pool. Beaton posed the Queen for two hours in all sorts of outfits except anything remotely Persian. He wrote:

> I wished to try to photograph the Queen looking like the Persian miniatures that were made during the golden age of Shah Abbas – the contemporary of Queen Elizabeth, under whom a Renaissance of Persian Art flourished. We had the sitter, the rose, and the pots of geraniums, but not the clothes. Surely there are materials to turn into a turban, a lot of jewels and a heavily embroidered Persian coat? An old woman servant brought an armful of Riviera foulards and garments trimmed with swansdown or ostrich feathers. 'We have a large garden party hat upstairs.' No, never mind. It was my mistake. How unwise to try and link the past with the present.[24]

After Tehran Beaton flew to Baghdad where he took portraits of the seven-year-old King Feisal. The pictures are commendable, Beaton being quite taken with the manners and demeanour of the young King, who had been raised by an English nanny.

> The child enjoyed changing the films in my camera and watching my impromptu methods, such as putting one table on top of another to act as an improvised tripod. Generally I feel loth to end most sittings; but for once I felt we had really got more than we needed, and the Prime Minister was awaiting his appointment to be photographed, so we said good-bye to the child with such a remarkable destiny.[25]

He then went on to Palestine, which was under British mandate. Besides photographing a number of religious leaders he took random snapshots, such as the one of a boy playing with a hoop in the ancient streets of Jerusalem (84). These pictures, too, had a place in the Ministry of Information's scheme of things, for one of its roles was to familiarise the British with the different cultures of their allies and vice versa. Next he travelled to Amman, the capital of Transjordan, where he photographed the ruler, Emir Abdullah. He met Glubb Pasha and men of the Arab Legion which he commanded. He also went to Syria and Lebanon.

Whenever possible, Beaton visited the antiquities of the regions. For the ardent traveller and sightseer the ancient ruins had a special significance during the war. One of the most moving passages in his book, *Near East*, is his description of the remains of ancient civilisation and the profound effect they had on him.

> God is sometimes very good, and to-day He gave me a present of Baalbek . . . Like Nimrod, the great grandson of Noah, who is the legendary founder of the first city to be built on this site, the early history of Baalbek is lost in mystery . . . So the stones of Baalbek go back to the days of men who had seen the sons of Noah. More than 2,000 years later, those stones were once more incorporated in the Temple of Jupiter, and the rough monoliths became the noble pillars we saw to-day, their capitals a mass of delicate carving and varied ornamentation . . . In the centuries which have passed over it, Baalbek has withstood two major earthquakes, the attacks of the Crusaders, the siege by Saladin, and the victory of Tamerlane in the fifteenth century.[26]

Beaton does not draw a parallel between the ancients and ourselves but the implication is there. He has tapped a most subtle form of propaganda without saying a word he did not fervently believe. In his appreciation of the beauty of Baalbek Beaton had asked what makes a civilisation great, strong and enduring. To reflect on the past is necessarily to contemplate the future and what Beaton so successfully achieves in his book is a reminder that we are not only living for today or to win the next battle, but like our forefathers since pre-Biblical times we have a destiny and a purpose for our existence.

When Beaton returned to Cairo on 25 June the city was astir with news of the possibility of an imminent German invasion. Typically, he imagined the worst: he would be stranded at Shepheard's Hotel when the Germans marched in. In fact, he was among the first to get permission to leave, and travel was arranged for him back to England via Nigeria and Portugal.

The Ministry wanted pictures of Nigeria, the largest of Britain's African colonies, and he delighted in photographing it from a purely aesthetic point of view.

. . . Some of the women carrying bunches of frangipani, or clusters of squawking hens, fled from the camera. One woman threw some water at me while others hid behind stacks of plates; but a crowd of excited children longed to be taken and they cheered each time I clicked the camera. It was a strange Pied Piper's progress surrounded by about fifty naked piccaninnies who clapped and shouted in unison.[27]

By 10 July he was in the opulent setting of wartime neutral Portugal which he described as 'the refuge of the "rats" ' where 'the richest of the collaborators . . . come . . . to do their deals.' Soon he learned what he was supposed to do.

The Ministry of Information have at last telegraphed that they wish me to photograph the entire Cabinet and all local celebrities. They have sent a list of proposed sitters ranging from the President to Salazar, from admirals to cardinals. I cannot think this can be of much help to anyone, and it is certainly of no 'importance'; but it will provide me with a contrast to the recent pictures I've been taking.[28]

But Beaton was tired out. The pictures of these sitters lack lustre. Perhaps the complacency of the Portuguese annoyed him more than he realised. He made one dull picture after another. Only at the bull-fight did he come alive, enjoy himself and photograph with imagination (89–90). When he finished his last assignment he dropped his Rolleiflex – the one and only camera he had with him throughout the whole Middle East tour – on a marble staircase and knew it was time to go home.

England

Returning to London in late summer 1942 Cecil Beaton was swept up once again in a whirlwind of creative and social activity. Before the end of his first week back, he was at Buckingham Palace with lights and large camera photographing the Royal Family with their distinguished visitor, Mrs Franklin Delano Roosevelt. The pictures appeared in the press at the end of October.

Although Beaton had thought it would be appropriate for him to find a full-time war job, in fact the balance between working for the Ministry of Information, photographing the Royal Family, doing a limited amount of fashion and portrait photography, designing theatre sets and costumes, and writing his books was the best of all possible arrangements. In *Photobiography* he mentions that it took him nearly all of 1943 to catch up on the captioning of his Middle Eastern negatives and writing notes and reports. He also did the décor and costumes for *Heartbreak House* with Edith Evans; the relief for Beaton to have at least a temporary escape from the war and to work with one of his favourite actresses was an obvious joy. The book he wrote that year, *Near East*, is descriptive and lively, a combination of story-telling and travel narrative. He departs from his more usual style of diary entry and gives an excellent account of the situation in the Middle East and of the men fighting the battles.

The Ministry of Information continued to send Beaton on assignments in Great Britain and behind the scenes there was talk of perhaps another foreign trip. Correspondence between Hugh Francis and Beaton in April 1943 shows that Beaton was photographing on Tyneside and was about to work for the Ministry of Health on themes relating to hospitals and nurseries. His photographs were being used in books, such as V S Pritchett's *Build the Ships* and a history of the Women's Auxiliary Air Force called *Wings on her Shoulders* by Katharine Bentley Beauman, and pamphlets, such as *Bomber Command*, published by the MOI. Hugh Francis was also arranging for some special exhibitions of his pictures. But Beaton, perhaps because he had had such an intense and exciting time in the Middle East or because wartime Britain was indeed bleak and there were shortages everywhere, longed to travel again.

Towards the end of 1943 the Ministry proposed that he should go to the Far East, to India and China, to gather material on these under-publicised theatres of war. They insisted that 'any contract should have safeguards against published references by Mr Beaton to the Ministry'. To enable him to carry out this demanding assignment the post of Special Photographer was created by the Ministry; Beaton was its first and only occupant. In December 1943 he received his orders to leave.

Burma and India

... the Dakota aboard which I took off from Land's End in the middle of the coldest night ever known, developed engine trouble as soon as it was air-borne and bucketed about the sky, shaking its terrified occupants like dice in a box, before crashing and bursting into flames. I was able to jump out at the last moment, but all my luggage perished ... My second attempt, however was successful, and a few days after I had arrived in Delhi my Rolleiflex and films were safely delivered to me, and I was sent off to photograph the war on the Assam–Burma front.

Visually so different from the Libyan campaign, this type of warfare proved almost as difficult to portray photographically. My pictures gave an almost idyllic impression of sunlight filtering through the tropical trees onto Gurkhas camouflaged with leaves and exotic plants as for a festival; but they gave not even the slightest hint of the loneliness and quiet terror of jungle warfare, which first and foremost is a war of nerves, never allowing complete relaxation, so that even during the long night hours men must lie with one ear cocked, listening to the rustle of the elephant grass and attempting to distinguish between the sound of a breaking twig and an approaching footfall. At any moment a Japanese sniper might creep through the branches, to appear five feet away with a knife raised above his head.[29]

Cecil Beaton was now in the Burmese jungle, nearer to actual combat and facing more physical discomfort than at any previous time. He never became a front-line cameraman, but he was close enough to be in possible danger and saw the casualties as they were brought back to camp. The men fighting in the Burmese campaign thought of themselves as the Forgotten Army. Many British soldiers had been stationed there for six or seven years and few journalists had covered their story. Their battles were not news. They welcomed Beaton enthusiastically and were delighted by his civilian suit after having seen nothing but khaki for months. Already he felt his trip to the Far East was worthwhile as his presence proved to these men that Whitehall had not forgotten them.

The two photographs that open the picture section on Burma and India (92–93) show wounded men being carried as gently as mothers cradle babies. Drained of all energy, their strong Gurkha faces express weariness and resignation. This is Beaton at his best. How poignant it is for one man to lay his cheek on the head of another, for one man to carry the full weight of the other. The charge into battle has been immortalised by painters, playwrights, composers and photographers. Beaton has shown the return of the wounded in images of beauty.

I was ready to start the day's work each morning at sunrise, visiting nearby camps in the mountains, photographing men in remote gun sites, electrical engineers at the wireless units; then off in a jeep over hazardous mountain passes. Everywhere I went I wrote down the names and addresses of the men who appeared in the photographs and promised to send them a picture. By the end of the day I was dazed with sleepiness in the unaccustomed mountain air and physically exhausted by the exercise of negotiating the precipitous slopes, but I looked with satisfaction at the hundreds of captions in which my day's work was recorded . . .

In a week I had acquired an enormous bundle of exposed negatives; and it was necessary to travel as light as possible, for the day's work entailed much hard going, crossing rivers in small boats, scrambling through undergrowth, or climbing up steep mountainsides. I decided I would rid myself of the unnecessary burden; and by giving my films to the press-relations officer who escorted me and letting him send them back for processing to HQ in Delhi, I made one of the greatest mistakes of my career. I never saw the film again.[30]

For years the incident plagued Beaton. The plane had not crashed, someone had just mishandled the films. The two aspects that troubled him most were that he had promised so many people pictures (he always kept his word on this) and that, as he wrote, 'they were taken while I was in full possession of my first enthusiasm and energy.'

He next flew further south to the Arakan front. Everywhere he went memoranda preceded him and he was always warmly received. Often an officer recognised his name and remarked, for example, how much his wife admired his pictures in *The Tatler*. By the time he had completed his work in this grim hinterland he 'returned in almost holiday mood to the comparatively peaceful atmosphere of India' where he stayed at the homes of the very rich, had an abundant number of servants to look after him and ate the best food.

Beaton found India an idyllic place to photograph.

. . . from the moment our seaplane glided down on to the Sacred Lake of Rajsammand, and I received my first glimpse of India, I had known that I would not be disappointed. The glittering white palaces of Udaipur towered in the distances: a small boy, in white and scarlet, wearing an enormous turban, came down the flower-potted terraces with a platter of highly coloured refreshments. I longed to start, then and there, on my photographic mission . . . I knew that photographing in India would be an endless pleasure.[31]

What is remarkable in the above paragraph and in much of his writing about India is the absence of any suggestion that it was wartime and that he was there for any purpose other than sightseeing, visiting the aristocracy and taking some photographs. There was in fact confusion between Beaton and the MOI about his mission in India since the fighting there was confined to the remote north-eastern frontier. When London finally saw the complete set of Indian pictures he was already in China. They requested he return to India for a couple of months to make more pictures of the everyday life of the Indian people.

Cecil Beaton's Indian photographs taken before and after his trip to China fall principally into four categories: formal portraits of the British rulers and Indian nobility; photographs of factories, hospitals and schools; military leaders and military activity, for example, training on the North West Frontier; and scenes of life in India.

The first category is well illustrated by the portrait of Lady Wavell on the stairs of Viceroy House in Delhi (109). Beaton took hundreds of what can best be described as fashion pictures. The official caption to this photograph mentions the fact that Lady Wavell is wearing a pale blue court dress. Whether it was on staircases, in throne rooms or in outdoor tropical gardens, Beaton employed his definitive style in photographing Maharajahs and Maharanees, Governor-Generals, their wives and children, and the Viceroy and his entourage. He was a master at lighting and backgrounds and these pictures look as if they were made for the society page; many were in fact later published in fashion magazines such as *Vogue*. His portraits are more revealing and effective when his subjects are doing something as, for example, the portrait of Lady Wavell making a radio speech (115) or Lord Wavell talking to two American soldiers (110).

To take so many rolls of film of Mary Colville, the daughter of Sir John Colville, or of Lady Wavell in various gowns was an indulgence on Beaton's part. But his brief from London included instructions to defend the record of the Empire. Nationalism was spreading in India and the MOI wanted pictures that showed the British Raj, and especially its rulers, to best advantage. Beaton wrote that 'the five generations of English service must command our respect' and proceeded to photograph in a manner consistent with that sentiment. Whether he achieved this goal in his elegant and haughty portraiture of the ruling class is hard to judge.

Photographing in hospitals, schools and factories is extremely difficult. There is little control over lighting or backgrounds. The photographer has the choice only of camera angle, subject and composition. Beaton, having had similar experience on the home front, handled the assignments imaginatively and created stories within the single frame. The finest example is the picture of Lieutenant Philip Ashley and the actress Miss Doreen Lawrence from ENSA (124). More like a still from a Hollywood movie than a slice of real life, Ashley becomes the perfect romantic hero, cigarette in hand, book open but set aside, left hand classically positioned, profile strong, with a young woman sitting on the edge of his bed. One longs to see him in uniform, in action, kissing his true love, leading his men into battle. Beaton knew better than most photographers which faces to select. His years in Hollywood helped and his affair with Greta Garbo reminds us of his preoccupation with physical beauty. In schools, in factories and in hospitals the people Beaton chose to photograph have strong features and faces rich in character. He would not show anyone at a disadvantage. He was remarkably respectful even to beggars on the street. He did not humiliate people or make them look ridiculous or pathetic. He was a gentleman photographer.

Beaton was sent to the North West Frontier and the Khyber Pass to photograph military patrols and training. Typical of this work and similar pictures he took in China is a distancing of himself from his subjects. He lets the landscape predominate and we see the scene as if from a balcony. Individual soldiers become part of the overall pattern and are indistinguishable from one another.

His photographs of officers differ from his other portraits in that he tended to get closer, use a sharper focus and make the generals and colonels appear large and rugged. If strength of character is what the Ministry of Information wanted in their photographs, Beaton's pictures, of which the one of General Auchinleck is an excellent example (107), achieve just that. On the other hand, the portrait of Admiral Lord Louis Mountbatten (106) is romantic but he, with his Royal connections, was not an ordinary military man.

The fourth category is the most interesting as Beaton was free to photograph any aspect of Indian life he chose. They give us new insights into Beaton in addition to showing a more complete picture of India. We see a sense of humour (Sikhs and Moslems receiving motor instruction (115)), a compassion for the poverty-stricken (a Bengali woman and child (117)) and an ability to spot the coincidental (men on a tram, every other one with his arm raised (98)). He could stand back like any visitor and watch life in a strange land unfold ((118) and (119) of tenement buildings in Bengal and villagers washing clothes) but his understanding of composition and form far excelled that of the average tourist.

There are two photographs in the book of peasants washing clothes and their differences are significant. The one in India (119) is taken from above, the figures small and lithe. Indian women were, for Beaton, 'like lotus flowers' and the people had 'extraordinary natural dignity'. There is no suggestion in the picture of crowding, of masses of people. India is a country, according to Beaton's vision, where each individual has room to move gracefully. China, on the other hand, swarms with bustling people, and the peasants are solidly rooted on strong, thick legs to the soil. The photograph of Chinese villagers washing clothes (154) is taken close-up from ground level looking down on the crouching, kneeling bodies. Beaton saw Chinese peasants 'working out their God-appointed destiny with deft hands and a patience that is touching'. One can feel their weight, the strength in their bodies. Whereas the Indians for Beaton have a mystical beauty, the Chinese are earthbound and hardworking.

Beaton was in India and Burma from January to April 1944 when he left for a two and a half month journey to China. He returned to India in June for one month to complete his photographic assignments before hitching his way on aircraft to Miami and New York City. Although while in India he complained of being 'uncomfortable, dirty and tired and doing things that do not normally interest me', generally he led quite a luxurious life. China was a different story.

China

After a frightening flight over the 'Hump' (the Himalayas), Cecil Beaton arrived shaken but safe in Chungking, the wartime capital of China. From there he would begin a five-thousand-mile lorry, sampan, train and air journey that would take him to every corner of Free China. He accompanied the Commander of the British Military Mission to China, General Gordon Grimsdale, on a tour of the forward areas. The MOI had mixed feelings about the work he was doing and privately wondered if the project was worthwhile and whether the expense of sending an 'artist' who often made awkward demands was in the best interests of a wartime nation. In May 1944 he received the following telegram:

> Please convey following message to Cecil Beaton from Francis Photographs Division. We have now received final consignment of Indian and first Chinese negatives. Processing shows considerable improvement but still not perfect. While captioning is adequate more detail on captions of Chinese pictures would be appreciated. Three hundred SEAC negatives still unarrived. Have made preliminary reviews all Indian material received and find too high a percentage British personalities and portraits and while appreciating necessity for proportion of these trust Chinese material will be predominantly Chinese showing especially life and war effort of the people. Most serious gaps in Indian series lack of typical village life scenes schools hospitals and social services featuring Indians . . .[32]

Beaton was the only civilian photographer the MOI sent to the Far East. The cost of supplying him with film, handling and processing it, and meeting all his expenses was no trivial matter. Jolts to Beaton in the form of frequent telegrams did have a positive effect. The Chinese photographs are more varied than the Indian ones and show a greater concern for the people. He did not shoot roll after roll on a single eminent or especially attractive person. For example, he took only a few exposures of Madame Sun Yat-sen, the charming widow of the founder of the Chinese republic. Pressures from the Ministry limited Beaton's artistic licence to some extent, but they also disciplined him.

The China pictures are for the most part more down to earth than his Indian ones. In India Beaton spent whole days at palaces engaged in small talk and banqueting. In China the weather was wet, the roads bumpy and accommodation at the outposts uncomfortable. It is no wonder he saw the human conditions more clearly.

> Every small town and village we stay in is redolent of disease. I am bitten by fleas which, I can only trust, are not plague carrying. Each night I go to bed anticipating visitors from the insect world. I think and dream of long baths in Calcutta . . .
> My luggage has now become a pitiable mess. My bag, made for air travel, does not protect any of its contents. The vibration of the truck has caused all the tubes of cream (tooth, shaving and cold) to twist their caps and become perforated; paints have oozed on to cotton-wool, socks, ties and medicine bottles; my one pair of pyjamas is soused in petrol; no article of clothing remains undamaged.[33]
> . . . Wherever I looked there were unattractive sights; women disembowelling animals or pulling the skin off eels, squatting to relieve themselves on the rice fields while they picked their noses or searched in their children's hair for vermin.[34]

After weeks of travelling and photographing he commented wryly:

> Returning to the same house in Chungking I vacated aeons of time ago, everything looks so much more luxurious. My standards of comfort have changed. Attuned to such poverty, to find a few unexpected, forgotten treasures in my bag left behind – a half-filled cigarette tin, a pot of shaving cream and a fresh shirt – this is a Croesus hoard![35]

Cecil Beaton was a difficult man, neither even-tempered nor by nature cooperative. Although he enjoyed being thought of as 'a sport' and knew that in wartime 'selfishness is the exception', he admitted clinging to his 'selfish civilian interests'. The rough existence in China made him rather 'morbid and introspective'. But even though he was aware of such tendencies, he still knew that the kind of photography he must do called for the keenest possible observation of the people and events around him. Beaton generally succeeded in anything he set out to do and always aimed to do it better than anyone else. No matter what reservations Hugh Francis and the staff of the Photographs Division might have had about Beaton's wartime photography, time has proved that he fulfilled his duties exceptionally well and created some profound and substantial images.

No photographs have more psychic energy than those of mothers and children in hospital wards. Those eyes look beyond earthly experience, as if the mother in one and the child in the other had a vision so profound that neither was quite of this world any longer. The mother resting with her son touches ever so gently the boy, whose eyes reveal a knowledge she does not possess (157). The mother in the other picture (155) looks as if she has already seen death and has become one with her child, as if he were still in the womb. They lie there suffering from the same disease.

Children's eyes continue to dominate the picture of a beggar picking over rags (159), a child with inflammation of the pancreas (158) and Li She-chan, son of Lieutenant-General Li Mo-an (130). In all three, the young boys seem worldly and mature. The son looks more intelligent than the father, the beggar sits like a direct descendant of a Chinese emperor, and the boy in the hospital with his thin arms and sensitive face should be playing the lead role in a dramatic performance. How different these are compared with the picture of little Eileen Dunne, who in her English hospital bed is all innocence and bewilderment.

Beaton's pictures of children pretending to be asleep (141–142) make them appear weightless, as if they could float up like petals in a breeze. The photograph of the boy printer (137) is a study of his bird-like, delicate hands as they work a large machine. Hands that are strong and healing are those of the English nurse holding the bruised head of a Chinese air raid casualty (156). His hands, too, are expressive and the grouping of the three has a religious quality.

Beaton employed three particular photographic techniques to make his Chinese pictures strong. One was capturing the play of light on a subject so that it looked almost bejewelled. There is the boy with the fan over his head, light falling on his nose and on his chest (140). The streaks of sunlight look like a painter's brush strokes. Another is the man on a Chengtu street, his face a mask of sunlight (139). The women packing cigarettes are studded with light and they and their work are half hidden, half revealed (136). The man stitching American flags simultaneously sews light into a nearly perfect oval (138). The earliest photographers in the nineteenth century talked about painting with light. Beaton never forgot this.

If he saw a strong geometric shape, such as a circle or a square, he would make it a central part of the composition. This was his second technique. He employed it in the desert when he used a burnt-out tank as a peephole through which to view other fragments looming in the sand like a conceptual work of art. The pictures of the ARP Headquarters in Chengtu (129) and of the Chinese commandos in training (126) use the same device.

Two of the finest photographs in the Chinese section are taken in Kweilin but have very different moods. One focuses on a solitary man in Western dress against a typical Chinese landscape (149) and the other is of a crowded scene with rickshaws, coolies carrying water, mothers with children on their backs, well-dressed businessmen, street vendors, telegraph poles and wooden houses (150). What the two photographs have in common is that they each look like a scene from a film. The lighting for both is perfect, as is the composition. In both, the story seems interesting. This is the third technique Beaton used in his photography: romanticising scenes of real life to fit cinematic criteria.

There is variety and contrast in the Chinese photographs. Beaton made sharply focused portraits against clean white walls strikingly marked with a horizontal and vertical line (143) and he made imperfectly focused landscapes from moving trains (153). But always he was drawn to the peasants.

The farmer, almost naked, with legs as muscular as Nijinsky's and wide apart as a wrestler's, plants in the swamps, with zealous speed, the small aigrettes of rice shoots. The water-treaders at the wheels, covered with sweat, defy by the hour the laws of gravity and cause water to run uphill. Stolid young women weed in the mire, or thresh vigorously throughout the heat of the day; children, with a wisp of bamboo, drive the herds of goats and gaggles of geese; the old women pick the leaves off the tea-trees, or tie little bags, against the onslaught of birds, over the ripening plums. The river coolies, in the rain, wearing the short capes of palm-tree fibre that, although of a design thousands of years old, are distinctly fashionable, strain at every limb as they fight the unpredictable currents and the evil spirits beneath the water.[36]

For others, might in war was measured in aircraft, guns and tanks. For Cecil Beaton, might was measured in muscle and the look in the eyes of children and generals, mothers and front-line soldiers. These latter armaments of war are at the heart of Cecil Beaton's wartime photographs.

Conclusion

Beaton returned to England from the Far East via New York. It was there that he learned of the liberation of Paris on 25 August 1944. After nearly a year away, London in September 1944 was still bleak. Rubble was everywhere, there were food shortages and the German V-bomb campaign was at its height. Often, as Beaton wrote, these weapons fell on 'poor inoffensive streets which contain no more important a target than the pub at the crossroads'.

He continued to undertake commissions for the Ministry of Information. Now, however, these 'propaganda' jobs in Jarrow, Nottingham or Bradford bored him. The European war was nearly over; it was for him a time to evaluate what had been, to start anew.

Hugh Francis, the vigorous and imaginative Director of the Photographs Division, was once again able to channel Beaton's creative energy into the service of the MOI. In October Francis asked him to organise an exhibition in Paris of photographs taken in Britain during the past four years. The object was to show the French what they had been unable to see during the German occupation: how the British had endured and fought during those long years since the fall of France and the evacuation from Dunkirk.

One of Beaton's finest qualities was the sincerity with which he involved himself in new challenges. He spoke of the exhibition as a 'thrilling assignment' and sorted through thousands of photographs which he and other press and service cameramen had taken to select the most telling historical documents. Although throughout the war he never worked as part of a team, now he revelled in the knowledge that he had helped, with others, to make an enduring record of the war. He found a gallery off the Champs Elysées, hung red velvet from floor to ceiling and proudly presented these pictures.

Beaton's war photographs come as a surprise, a most extraordinary surprise in the context of his other work. They are a superb achievement and compel us to recognise the breadth of his talent. He loved to photograph, to put a frame around an aspect of the world he found intriguing. He was fascinated with patterns and shapes, gestures and faces, and with his perceptive eye was able to translate subtle details into vivid pictures.

His story of the Second World War is subjective. His knowledge of how to light a face, create a dramatic background, spot a symbolic action, humanise a sitter, see beauty, use abstraction, arouse sympathy and compose a picture ensured that this body of work was varied and stimulating. The mood of the photographs changes according to what Beaton thought proper in a certain situation, according to how he felt. Some of the work combines to produce a coherent statement, as in his series on the Royal Air Force. The Chinese and Indian photographs, however, seem amorphous as a group, but are individually powerful.

For forty years all but a celebrated few of Cecil Beaton's Second World War photographs have been largely ignored. We now have the opportunity to learn about this important facet of his career and to view the years from 1940 to 1944 through the images of this master photographer.

GAIL BUCKLAND

References

1 Cecil Beaton, *Self Portrait with Friends*, ed. Richard Buckle (London, 1979), pp. 421–2
2 Cecil Beaton, *Air of Glory* (London, 1941), p. 7
3 Cecil Beaton, *The Best of Beaton* (London, 1968), p. 133
4 Cecil Beaton, *The Years Between* (London, 1965), p. 11
5 MOI papers, Imperial War Museum
6 *The Best of Beaton*, p. 115
7 *War Pictures by British Artists: Production*, second series, introduction by Cecil Beaton (London, 1943), pp. 5–7
8 James Pope-Hennessy and Cecil Beaton, *History under Fire* (London, 1941), p.vi
9 *The Years Between*, p. 87
10 *Ibid*. p. 86
11 Cecil Beaton, *Winged Squadrons* (London, 1942), p. 6
12 *Ibid*. p. 29
13 Cecil Beaton, *Air of Glory* (London, 1941), p. 7
14 *Ibid*. p. 8
15 *The Years Between*, p. 134
16 Cecil Beaton, *Near East* (London, 1943), p. 1
17 *Ibid*. p. 9
18 *The Years Between*, p. 136
19 *Ibid*. p. 135
20 *Ibid*. p. 144
21 Cecil Beaton, *Photobiography* (New York, 1951), pp. 144–6
22 *Near East*, p. 57
23 *The Years Between*, pp. 157–8
24 *Near East*, p. 101
25 *Ibid*. p. 108
26 *Ibid*. p. 124
27 *The Years Between*, p. 192
28 *Ibid*. p. 197
29 *Photobiography*, p. 154
30 *Ibid*. pp. 157–8
31 Cecil Beaton, *An Indian Album* (London, 1945–6), introduction
32 Telegram, MOI to British Embassy, Chungking, 27 May 1944. The Estate of Cecil Beaton.
33 *The Years Between*, p. 309
34 Cecil Beaton, *Far East* (London, 1945), p. 83
35 *The Years Between*, p. 319
36 *Ibid*. p. 325

The Home Front

Most of Cecil Beaton's official assignments in the United Kingdom were carried out during 1940 and 1941, perhaps the most difficult years of the war for Britain. The conflict engulfed the whole population. Whether conscripted into the services, directed into industry or evacuated to the country the lives of men, women and children were fundamentally changed. In addition, when the Blitz began in September 1940 civilians found themselves in the front line. The photographs which Beaton took during this period show the spirit of the British people under fire, damage to historic buildings, the mobilisation of Britain's industrial and military resources, and the Royal Air Force, which had warded off the threat of invasion and was now Britain's sole means of striking directly at Germany. Beaton also portrayed the country's leaders, notably the Prime Minister and the Royal Family, who symbolised the nation's defiance at this time of peril.

1

Spring planting in Wiltshire in 1940.

2

The western bell towers of St Paul's Cathedral
after the heavy incendiary raid on 29 December 1940.

3

Children evacuated from London in 1939 billeted at
Wilton House, home of the Earl of Pembroke.

4

A bare hall at Buckingham Palace in 1941 with buckets
to catch water from the Blitz-damaged roof.

5

6

London bomb damage 1940–1: the mangled staircase of a Kensington house (5).
Dr Samuel Johnson's attic in Gough Square in the City (6).

7

8

The Card Room at White's Club in Westminster (7).
A store room at the Natural History Museum in South Kensington (8).

9

American servicemen in a London street in 1943.

A little girl, who was not evacuated from the city in 1939, imagines a country scene.

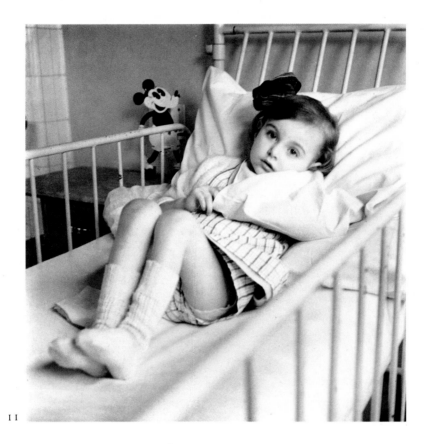

11

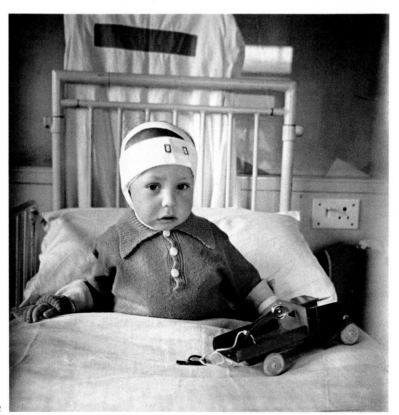

12

Air raid casualties in the Great Ormond Street Hospital
for Sick Children in London in 1940.

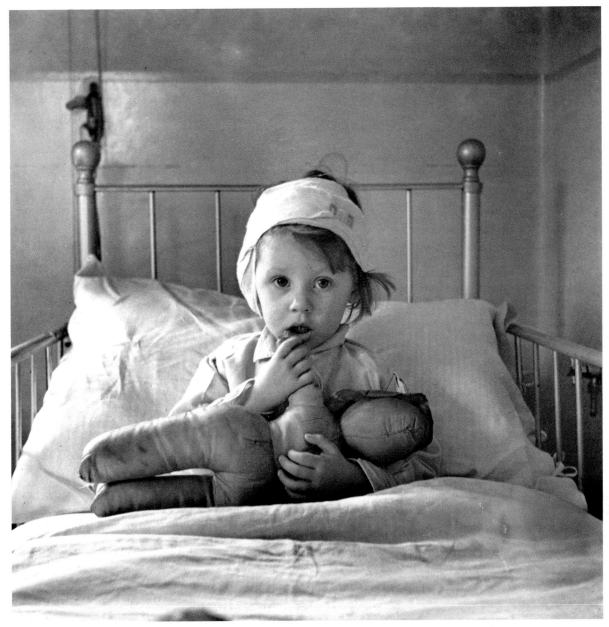

13

Three-year-old Eileen Dunne in the Hospital for Sick Children, 1940.

14

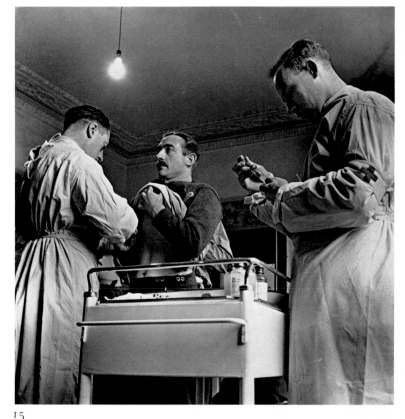

15

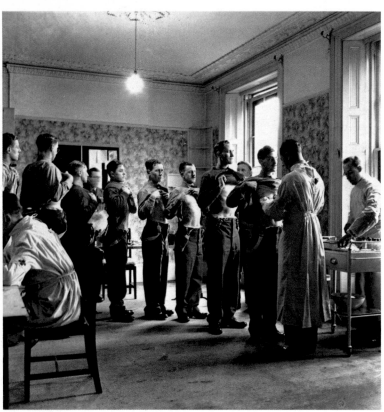

16

17

de Havilland Training School 1941: kit issue, medical
inspection and physical training for RAF cadets.

Junior airmen learning the skill of aircraft recognition.

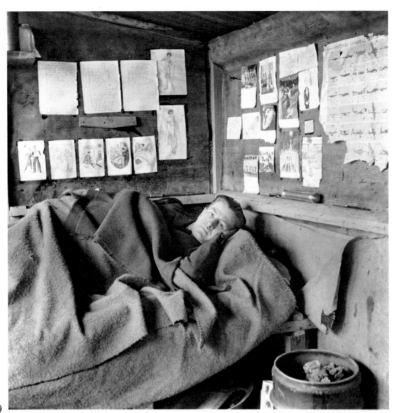

19

20

A mechanic waiting for the bombers' return (19).
A fighter pilot relaxing still wearing flying kit (20).

Pilot Officer James Daley DFC, an air 'ace' serving with
No.121 Squadron, RAF, one of the American 'Eagle' squadrons.

22

23

Fighter pilots of No.401 Squadron, RAF, outside their camouflaged flight office (22).
A young Hurricane pilot of No.249 Squadron, RAF (23).

Hurricane pilots of No.56 Squadron, R A F, exchange stories after a convoy patrol.

25

26

Bomber Command night attack 1941: loading the bombs (25).
Plotting the raiders' progress in the station operations room (26).

27

28

Waiting on the control tower (27).
Debriefing air crew after an operation (28).

29

The pilot and co-pilot of a Wellington bomber in 1941.

30

The rear gunner of a Wellington bomber.

RAF ground crew servicing an Airspeed Oxford.

Inside a barrage balloon members of the Women's Auxiliary
Air Force repair its thousand yards of fabric.

33

A recruit being interviewed for the Women's Royal Naval Service in 1940.

34

A newly commissioned officer of the Women's Auxiliary Air Force on parade in 1942.

A Wren officer posing with a ship's figurehead at Portsmouth Naval Base in 1940.

36

Wren wine stewards in the Painted Hall of the Royal Naval College, Greenwich, in 1940.

Two sailors feeding their cat in 1940 (37).
A veteran captain of the Royal Navy in 1941 (38).

A young sailor attending the torpedo training school at
HMS *Vernon*, a shore station at Portsmouth, in 1941.

40

A soldier manning an artillery direction finder
at a coastal battery.

41

42

Training on Salisbury Plain in 1940: firing a 25-pounder gun-howitzer (41).
Driving a Cruiser Mark III tank (42).

43

Soldiers keeping watch on the Channel in 1941.

44

Two of Beaton's friends, Lady Anglesey and her daughter
Lady Caroline Paget, in North Wales in 1940.

45

A welder in a Tyneside shipyard in 1943.

46

47

Workers preparing alloy in a foundry in 1940 (46).
A girl checking airscrew blades in 1940 (47).

The Prime Minister, Mr Winston Churchill, caught unawares
in the Cabinet Room at No.10 Downing Street in September 1940.

49

The Prime Minister, Mr Winston Churchill:
'He stared into my camera like a bulldog guarding its kennel.'

50

Mr Churchill's bedroom at No.10 Downing Street.

The hall at No.10, with Cabinet members' hats and coats on the side-table.

52

Lord Halifax, the Secretary of State for Foreign Affairs, in 1940.

53

King George VI, in Royal Air Force uniform, with Princess Elizabeth,
Princess Margaret and Queen Elizabeth at Windsor Castle in 1942.

General Dwight D Eisenhower, Supreme Allied Commander,
at his Versailles headquarters in 1945.

Colonel Charles de Gaulle, at the headquarters of the
Free French organisation in London in 1940.

56

Churchill and de Gaulle inspecting French troops on
the Vosges Front on 13 November 1944.

The Middle East

In March 1942, when Cecil Beaton arrived in Cairo, public attention in Britain was concentrated upon the dramatic campaign in North Africa, then the only theatre in which British and German troops were engaged. In 1941 Rommel's German and Italian army had swept through Libya, forcing the British to withdraw into Egypt; a counter-attack by the Eighth Army in November pushed Rommel back to the western borders of Cyrenaica and raised the siege of Tobruk. A four-month lull followed, which coincided with Beaton's visit to the desert front. Rommel attacked again in May 1942 but was finally halted less than 150 miles from Cairo by General Sir Claude Auchinleck at El Alamein, where in October General Montgomery was to win the decisive battle of the desert war. In June Beaton left Cairo and travelled to Iran, Iraq, Transjordan, Palestine, Syria and Lebanon. The photographs he took there were intended to familiarise the British public with these strategically important countries and their leaders.

On board HMS *Alcantara* en route to Sierra Leone:
the ship's company exercises to the music of the band.

58

59

A sailor doing some mending (58).
Off-watch, a sailor drowsing in the tropical sun (59).

60

Wreckage of Italian aircraft, probably near the
Halfaya Pass on the border of Egypt and Libya.

Remains of German tanks at Sidi Rezegh in Libya.

62

Airmen waiting for transport, always an unpredictable
quantity in the desert.

63

Camels, more reliable than mechanical equipment
in the sand, rolling a new runway.

Shadows on the sand underneath an RAF Beaufighter.

Lunchtime in a RAF officers' mess in Egypt
at a base some distance from the front.

66

A sandstorm in the desert.

A Sunderland flying boat of No.230 Squadron, RAF,
framed by the legs of an airman.

68

An officer of the Royal Tank Regiment.

69

Air Vice-Marshal Sir Arthur Coningham, the commander of the
Western Desert Air Force, outside his mobile headquarters.

70

The damaged roof of the fire station in Tobruk.

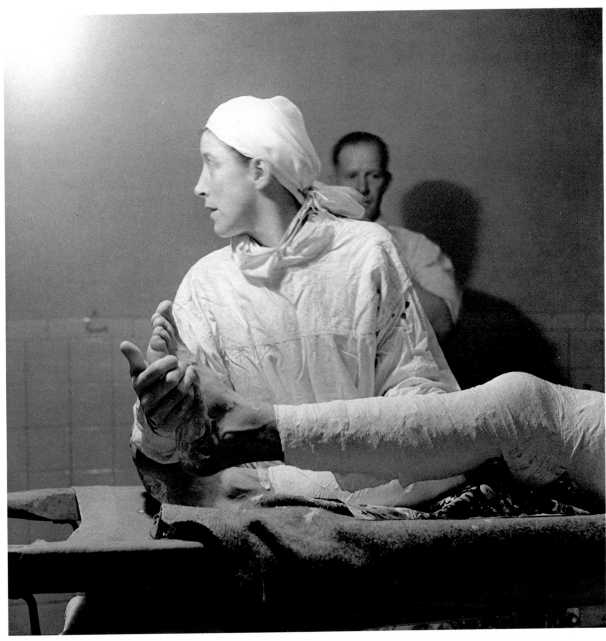

71

An army nurse helping in the operating theatre of
the General Hospital in Tobruk.

72

A Long Range Desert Group patrol at its headquarters at Siwa.

73

The mobile headquarters of an infantry battalion of
the New Zealand Division in the desert.

A driver peering out of his Grant tank.

75

A driver and gunner inside their Grant tank.

Abandoned Italian respirators in the sand.

A shattered Matilda tank daubed with the German slogan,
'Gone to its last home.'

78

79

The British Ambassador to Egypt, Sir Miles Lampson, and Lady Lampson (78).
Air Chief Marshal Sir Arthur Tedder,
commander of the R A F in the Middle East, with his Air Council in Cairo (79).

80

81

The entrance hall of General Headquarters, Cairo (80).
Colonel Philip Astley, an army public relations officer, in Cairo (81).

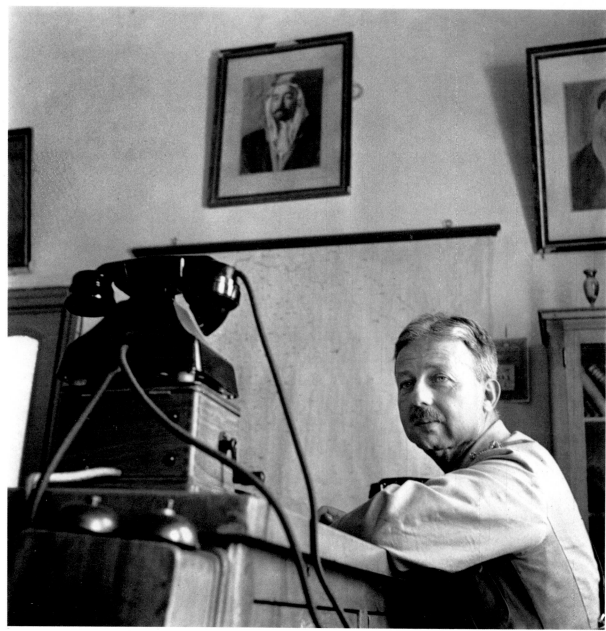

82

Brigadier Sir John Bagot Glubb, famous as Glubb Pasha,
the commander of the Arab Legion.

83

An Arab Legionnaire.

A young boy in the streets of Jerusalem.

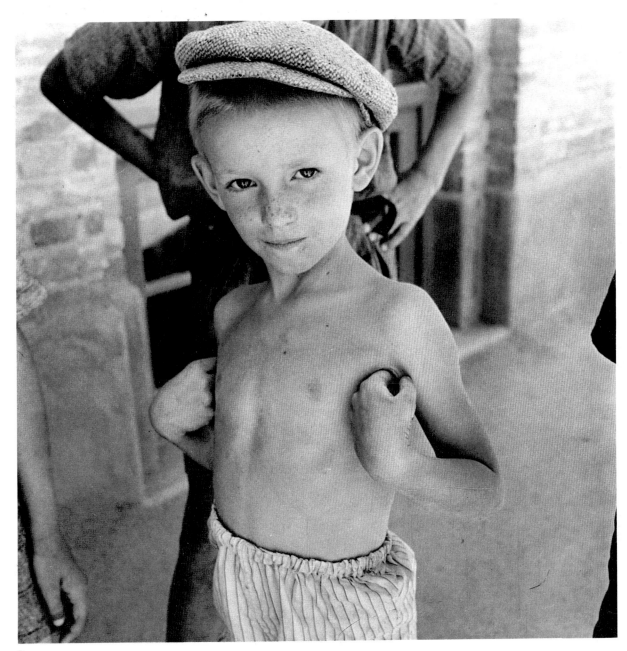

85

A young Jewish refugee from Poland in a camp in Palestine.

The Shah of Iran, Mohammed Reza Pahlevi, with his first wife, Queen Fawzieh,
and their daughter, Princess Chahnaz.

87

88

Seven-year-old King Feisal II of Iraq in the Palace of Flowers, Baghdad (87).
Emir Abdullah of Transjordan in his palace at Amman (88).

89

The bull-ring in Lisbon, where Beaton spent an afternoon watching the fighting.

Spectators dressed for the occasion at a Sunday bull-fight in Lisbon.

91

Three African boys chasing guinea fowl on the Nigerian coast near Lagos.

Burma and India

When Beaton visited the Burma front in January 1944 the Japanese High Command was making preparations for an advance into India. Since 1942 the Japanese and British forces had been locked in a vicious but inconclusive jungle war on the remote India–Burma frontier. Morale in the Fourteenth Army dramatically improved after the appointment of Major-General William Slim as its commander and Vice-Admiral Lord Louis Mountbatten as Supreme Allied Commander in South East Asia in late 1943. Slim's brilliant victory at the battle of Imphal–Kohima in July 1944 destroyed the myth of Japanese invincibility and paved the way for the reconquest of Burma. Within India the nationalist movement was gaining momentum but the British government refused to countenance the transfer of political power until after the war. Beaton's photographs give no hint of these tensions and concentrate instead on the splendour of the British Raj and the natural beauty he found in India and its people.

92

A sling improvised by Gurkha soldiers to carry the
wounded in the Chin Hills on the Burma Front.

A Gurkha soldier transporting a wounded man on his
back through the jungle.

94

Fighter pilots at a Royal Air Force base on the India–Burma
border showing some tribesmen over a Spitfire.

95

A young corporal lying in front of his camouflaged
Universal Carrier in the jungle on the Burma Front.

96

Soldiers gather for their evening meal in a camp high in
the Chin Hills.

97

A stranded army truck, a common plight of vehicles
travelling on the difficult roads of the Chin Hills.

Passengers on a crowded tram in Calcutta.

A driver cranking the engine of his ambulance
at an air raid precautions post in Calcutta.

Three stokers on the mess deck of the sloop HMIS *Sutlej*.

A clerk pointing to a chart of military training
films available from the main depot in Bombay.

102

A group of Punjabi women.

103

The Prime Minister of Jaipur, Sir Mizram Ismail.

104

Mr R G Casey, the Australian diplomat who became
Governor of Bengal, at Government House, Calcutta.

The Vicereine, Lady Wavell, broadcasting on behalf of the Red Cross.

Admiral Lord Louis Mountbatten,
Supreme Allied Commander in South East Asia.

107

General Sir Claude Auchinleck, Commander-in-Chief of the Indian Army.

108

Sir John Colville, Governor of Bombay, and Lady Colville,
enthroned in full regalia at Government House, Bombay.

109

Lady Wavell, standing on the grand staircase of the Viceroy's House in Delhi.

110

The Viceroy, Field-Marshal Viscount Wavell, talking to two
American soldiers in the grounds of the Viceregal Lodge at Simla.

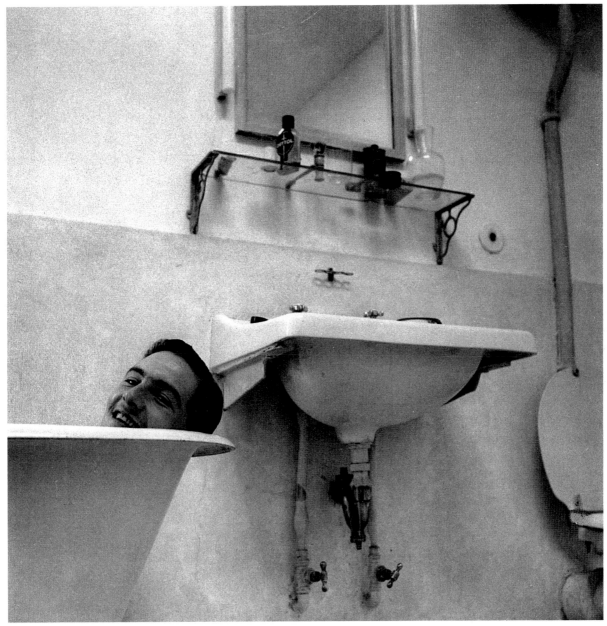

111

A gunner, Lieutenant Antony Liddell, enjoying a bath
at the leave camp on the Viceroy's estate at Simla.

112

Tochi Scouts, part of the frontier militia, clambering
up a mountain on the border between India and Afghanistan.

Troops of a Kashmir regiment on the Shagai
plateau near the eastern end of the Khyber Pass.

Sikh recruits, their turbans and belts discarded,
training at Nowshera military school near the North West Frontier.

115

Advanced recruits learning about engines at Nowshera military school.

An open-air class room in a village school.

A Bengali woman and child.

118

Cows lying placidly in the unmetalled street outside
the poor tenement buildings of a Bengali town.

A square by the river in a Bengali town where
the people gather to wash themselves and their clothes.

A boy in the Jain temple in Calcutta (120).
A Bengali village schoolboy (121).

A class at one of the oldest schools for girls in Bengal,
the Victoria Institute in Calcutta.

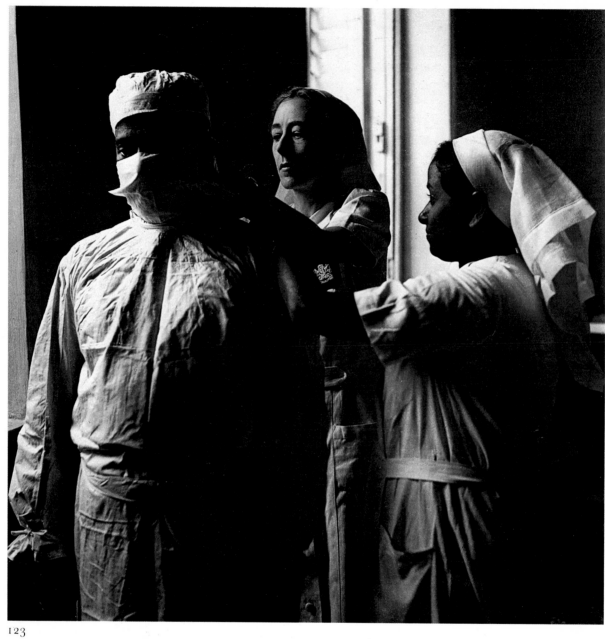

123

A British sister showing an Indian nurse how to adjust a
doctor's mask at a first aid post in Calcutta.

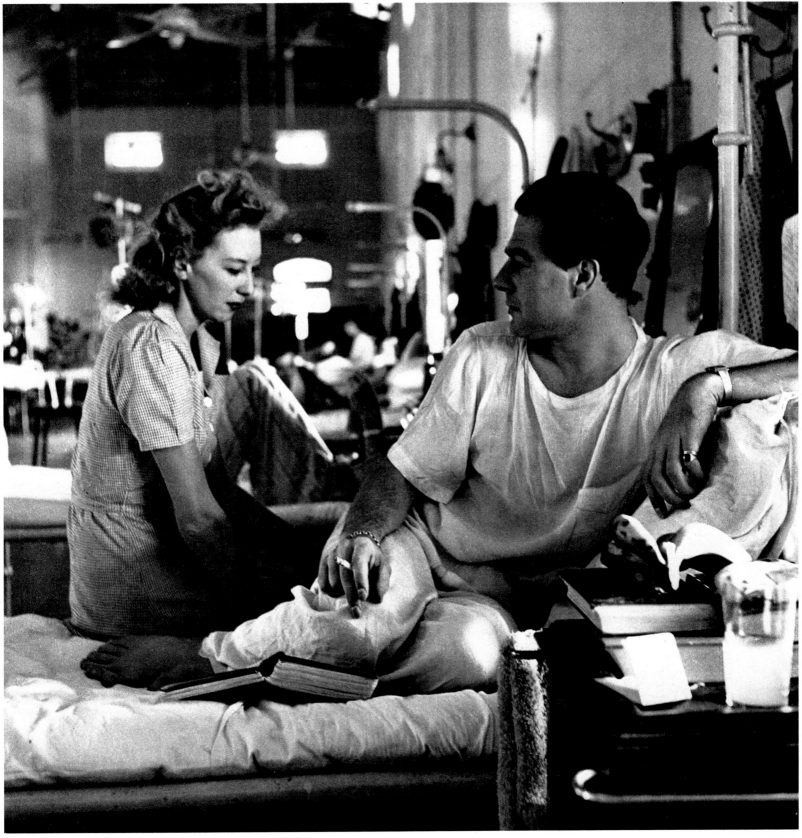

Lieutenant Philip Ashley, convalescing in a Bombay hospital, is visited by the actress Miss Doreen Lawrence from ENSA.

A Red Cross mobile tea wagon at Calcutta airport.

China

Japan had invaded China in 1937 and by the end of the following year had occupied the whole of the eastern seaboard, forcing the Nationalist government under Chiang Kai-shek to retreat inland to Chungking. Even before the Japanese attack on Pearl Harbor the United States had begun to supply Chiang Kai-shek with economic and military aid. President Roosevelt and his advisers saw China as an important member of the United Nations alliance – a view not shared by the British. In reality China was in a state of chaos, its government corrupt and tyrannical, its army disorganised and ill-equipped. Furthermore, the Communists from their strongholds in the north-west were waging a guerilla war against both the Japanese and the Nationalist forces. Beaton, who arrived in Chungking in April 1944, soon became aware of the country's plight. He made an extensive tour of the southern provinces of Szechwan, Hunan, Kwangsi, Fukien and Chekiang recording the army, the politicians and the people of China.

126

Chinese commando troops during an exercise in tactics at
Pihu military training centre in south-eastern China.

A young Chinese soldier in training as a commando.

A demonstration of the exercise dubbed 'The Heavenly Gate'
at Pihu military training centre.

The Chinese Police Force: the Assistant Chief of
Police and his staff at Chengtu in south-western China.

130

Lieutenant-General Li Mo-an, who entertained Beaton in his house at Pihu, with his son, Li She-chan.

131

Allied commanders in China: the American Major-General Claire Chennault
and his British colleague Major-General Gordon Grimsdale (behind).

132

133

Madame Sun Yat-sen, widow of the founder of the Chinese republic (132).
Lieutenant-General Wu Te-chen, Secretary-General of the Kuomintang (133).

Lieutenant-General Adrian Carton de Wiart vc, Mr Churchill's
special representative to the Kuomintang Government.

135

A girl wrapping cartons of cigarettes at
Nanyang Brothers' tobacco factory in Chungking.

Factory hands packing cigarettes at
Nanyang Brothers' tobacco factory in Chungking.

137

A Chinese boy at the Canadian Mission Press in Chengtu.

An enterprising Chinese craftsman making American flags in Chengtu.

139

A man's face caught in the sunlight in Chengtu.

140

A small boy posing with his fan in Chengtu.

141

A little girl having a mid-day rest at the Victoria Nursery School in Chungking.

142

Pupils, mostly the children of government officials who had fled from the Japanese, at a school in Chungking.

A cadet of the cavalry school of Yencheng University.

144

Cadets attending a lecture on government at Pihu military training centre.

145

A parade at the Central Military Academy in Chengtu.

A Chinese soldier practising guerilla tactics at
Pihu military training centre.

Chinese soldiers wearing gas masks at Pihu military training centre.

148

A demonstration of the martial arts at a physical training
college at Peipei in western China.

A scene on Chung Chin bridge in Kweilin in the southern
province of Kwangsi.

A street scene in Kweilin.

151

Onlookers gathering for a demonstration of air raid precautions
in Chungking.

Disabled soldiers learning to make oiled paper umbrellas
at a rehabilitation centre in Chungking.

153

Paddy fields in the central province of Hunan snapped through
a train window.

154

Women of a village in the south-eastern province of Fukien
washing their laundry in a stream.

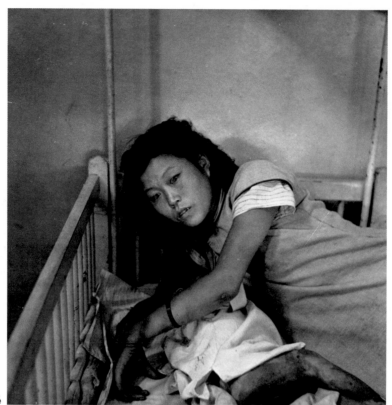

155

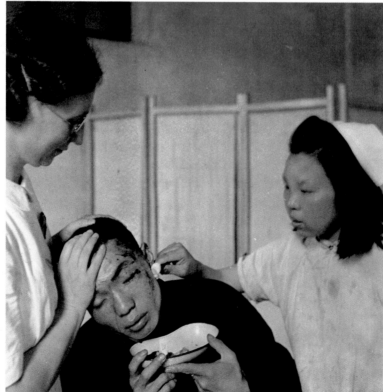

156

A sick mother and child in the Canadian Mission Hospital in Chengtu (155).
An air raid casualty at the Red Cross Hospital in Changsa (156).

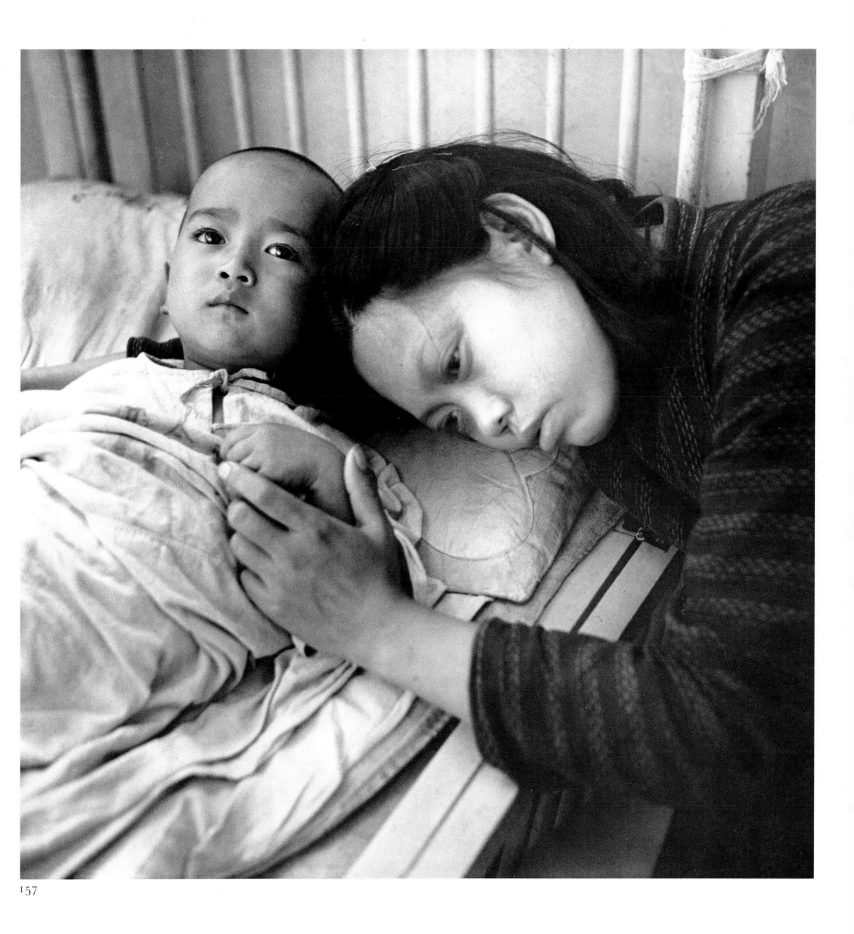

A mother resting by the cot of her sick child in the
Canadian Mission Hospital in Chengtu.

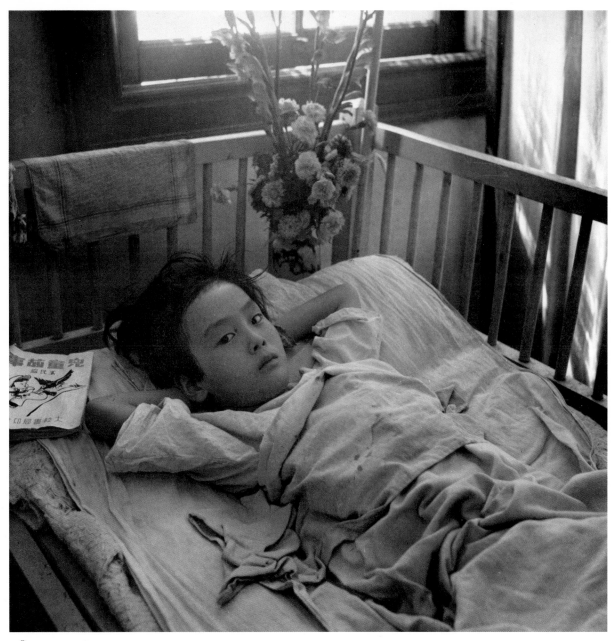

158

A patient in the children's ward of the Canadian Mission Hospital in Chengtu.

A destitute boy in the Poor People's Refuge in Changsa,
where refugees from occupied China were sheltered.

Rafts of bamboo at the river's edge in Kweilin, Kwangsi province.

161

Boys sawing pine logs in the Ming Sung naval dock yard in Chungking.

Soldiers sawing wood outside their barracks in Chengtu.

Notes on the Photographs

2
To Beaton's chagrin it was not his own version of this famous image of the Second World War which was published first. During his morning session he had been irritated by a press photographer dogging his footsteps. He wrote: 'Returning from lunch with my publisher, my morning's pictures still undeveloped in my overcoat pocket, I found the press photographer's picture was already on the front page of the Evening News.'

4
This photograph is part of the comprehensive photographic record of Buckingham Palace which Beaton was asked by King George VI and Queen Elizabeth to make in 1941. During the Blitz the Palace had received three direct hits and suffered considerable damage.

5–8
These photographs were taken for Beaton's survey with James Pope-Hennessy of bomb damage to London's historic buildings, published as *History under Fire* in 1941.

10
This little girl's parents had apparently ignored the government's advice to send children to the country at the outbreak of war. This first evacuation scheme was not a complete success: many children either did not leave the cities at all or, as the threatened raids did not come immediately, were soon brought back from the country by their parents.

13
Beaton wrote of this famous portrait of a young air raid victim: 'Her face, so babylike, had suddenly grown old and pale; and as I approached her bed, she looked at me in a trance of trustful misery.'

14–31
This group of photographs was taken during Beaton's study of the Royal Air Force in 1941. Among the bases he visited were the de Havilland Training School at Hatfield, the fighter stations at Biggin Hill, North Weald and Tangmere, and the bomber bases at Mildenhall and Waddington.

14–18
These photographs, taken at the de Havilland Training School, were published in the *Illustrated London News* on 22 March 1941 to illustrate an article describing the various stages of Royal Air Force training.

21
No. 121 Squadron, RAF, which became operational in May 1941, was the second of the three 'Eagle' squadrons of American volunteers serving with the Royal Air Force. Pilot Officer James Daley was awarded the Distinguished Flying Cross after shooting down his third enemy aircraft and destroying a minesweeper in the English Channel on 27 May 1942.

22–4
Beaton took these photographs with the idea of illustrating a typical day in the life of a fighter pilot. They were used in an article published in *The Sketch* on 16 April 1941. In *Winged Squadrons* he noted the differences he found between the pilots of Bomber and Fighter Command: 'The bomber pilots seem to possess a reserve born of their great responsibility to the crew. The fighter pilots are the gay, more reckless ones, more temperamental, perhaps a bit selfish, but only in comparison with the rest of the Royal Air Force, for selfishness as it is known in the outside world cannot exist here.'

25–30
This group of photographs of Bomber Command formed one of a number of 'feature sets' of pictures illustrating life in wartime Britain which the Ministry of Information prepared for general distribution at home and abroad.

29
This pilot of a Wellington bomber was exactly the type of youthful hero suitable for the Ministry's publicity. His anonymity was preserved but he was in fact nineteen-year-old Pilot Officer Geoffrey Fisher DFC of No. 149 (East India) Squadron, RAF, based at Mildenhall.

35
Beaton's photograph, which was reproduced in *The Sketch*, *Vogue* and the *Illustrated London News* in December 1940, symbolised the dignity and courage of women in their new wartime roles. It shows Second Officer Félicité Potter of the Women's Royal Naval Service posing with the replica of the nineteenth-century wooden battleship HMS *Queen Charlotte* at the naval gunnery school in Portsmouth.

37
The Sunday Chronicle and Referee published this photograph on 8 September 1940, emphasising its sentimental appeal with the caption 'These are the boys who risk their lives so you can get food.'

44
Beaton often used photographs which he took of his friends for publication. This one shows how in wartime drab clothing had become ubiquitous even for society ladies.

48
This famous portrait of Churchill was first published in the morning papers on 23 December 1940 to coincide with a radio broadcast that evening in which he roundly condemned Mussolini's policies.

51
The American magazine *Life* frequently used Beaton's work. This photograph was published in its issue of 27 January 1941 as part of a major feature on the British Prime Minister and his family. Great play was made of the fact that the Prime Minister's famous Homburg hat could be seen on the middle shelf of the side-table in the hall. Long before America's entry into the war in December 1941 *Life* was notably sympathetic to the British cause.

53
After the success of his portraits of Queen Elizabeth in 1939, Beaton was regularly summoned to Buckingham Palace or Windsor Castle for further photographic sessions. The Royal Family regarded Windsor as their main home and during the war the young Princesses spent virtually all their time there. Beaton wrote: 'Windsor Castle, vast and cold. The family were now living around the courtyard in the rooms built by George IV which has Gothic additions. There was a van delivering coal at the entrance at which we should have arrived, so I was taken to the service entrance and got an interesting glimpse of the vast underworld of scullion maids filling ancient-looking water bottles and creating an almost medieval effect of bustle.'

56
This picture was taken during Beaton's trip to France in November 1944 to organise the Ministry of Information's exhibition in Paris of photographs of the war. By then the Germans had been expelled from France and de Gaulle recognised as leader of the provisional French government.

60–1
These photographs were published in many magazines in 1942 and were later included in *Near East*. Their emotive power attracted considerable praise and they were seen as vindicating the Ministry's appointment of an 'artistic' photographer. Halfaya Pass, 65 miles east of Tobruk, was the scene of bitter fighting during Operation 'Battleaxe' in June 1941. Sidi Rezegh, 20 miles south-east of Tobruk, was fiercely contested in the 'Crusader' battles towards the end of 1941, changing hands five times.

62–9
This group of photographs was taken by Cecil Beaton in his capacity as an official RAF photographer in the Western Desert. Of the life there he wrote: 'Though it can be said that in all the world there can be no more wasteful, heartless, and purposeless theatre of war, a more unsuitable habitation for human beings, still the desert possesses its advantages. There can be no more healthy battle-ground. Most men are physically fitter than ever before. Life here is primeval. It is simple with the simplicity of the animals. Yet it seems from this simplicity springs a new contentment. In the desert men are contented, they become "sand happy".'

66
Quoting the advice of experienced desert campaigners, Beaton wrote of this scene: 'The storm of sand, which may continue for days, brings life to a standstill. "The only thing to do is wrap a towel around your head and sleep the sleep of hibernation until it is over".'

69
Beaton was impressed by Air Vice-Marshal Coningham: 'Here was living proof of the benefits to be derived from remaining in the desert as against the man who becomes affected by the climatic indolence of Cairo. Huge, good-looking, strong, sunburnt, like a peach in perfection, with a wide column of a neck, massive chest.' Beaton's portraits of senior officers were distributed by the Ministry of Information for use in newspaper and magazine profiles.

70
'Here was wreckage on a large and sinister scale,' wrote Beaton of Tobruk. 'Nothing remains altogether unscathed but the hospital still stands, and curiously enough, the towers of mosque and church rise serene above the débris of toppling walls.' An important supply port, Tobruk with its garrison of British, Australian, New Zealand and Polish troops had successfully withstood a ten-month siege in 1941.

74–5
Beaton took these photographs while visiting the 4th Armoured Brigade, a formation of the 7th Armoured Division, the 'Desert Rats'. The driver shown was named as Lance-Corporal Harry Zolk from London. The American-built Grant tank went into service with the Eighth Army in March 1942. Its 75-mm gun at last enabled the British to challenge the supremacy of the panzer divisions.

76
When General Montgomery launched his offensive at El Alamein on 8 October 1942 this photograph was published in *The Sketch* with the jubilant caption that these were 'useless Italian respirators flung away by their owners as they retreated from the British advance'. In fact the picture had been taken several months earlier.

78

Air Chief Marshal Tedder's officers are from left to right: Air Commodore K L Boswell, Air Vice-Marshals H E P Wigglesworth and G C Pirie, and Air Marshal R M Drummond. Although critical of the torpid atmosphere of GHQ Cairo, Beaton spoke highly of Tedder's industry and acumen, describing him as 'one of the hardest workers in the Middle East'.

82

Glubb Pasha devoted his life to furthering the community of British and Arab interests in the Middle East. He created Transjordan's army, the Arab Legion, and turned it into a crack fighting force. 'Quiet and self-effacing,' was Beaton's verdict. 'Nothing riles him more than to be called "The Second Lawrence".'

85

This boy was one of several thousand Poles who fled from Nazi persecution to Palestine during the war. Many more such refugees entered the country than the British had planned, so intensifying hostility between Arab and Jew.

86

The Sketch published Beaton's photographs of the Iranian royal family on 26 August 1942 with an article praising the Shah's western outlook, the Queen's beauty and the country's friendship with Britain.

87

Life, *Vogue* and the *Illustrated London News* all included pictures of the boy-king of Iraq in August 1942, together with homely stories about his English nanny and the model Hurricane the RAF mechanics in Iraq had given him for his birthday. In his diary of the war years, Beaton recounts that a mutilated copy of this photograph was found in the palace ruins when the King was assassinated in 1958.

88

Beaton wrote of his meeting with Emir Abdullah: 'Suddenly I found myself having to make all the conversational "running" to a nice old man, the brother of the late King Faisal, and grandfather of the present King of Iraq, with painted eyes, who smelt appetizingly of musk and looked very starched and clean in immaculate white shift and turban.'

91

One of Beaton's pastoral photographs of Nigeria, which was reproduced in *Vogue* in December 1942 in an article on West Africa. This region became an important stepping stone in Allied communications with the Middle East after the virtual closure of the Mediterranean in the spring of 1941.

92

In the series of articles which he wrote for the *Daily Mail* during his tour of India, Beaton described the Gurkhas of the Fourteenth Army as amongst 'the finest photographic subjects I have met'. The army had experienced considerable difficulty in organising efficient medical facilities in the jungle and Beaton's photographs show some of the makeshift practices in common use.

97

Beaton wrote of his own experience of travelling in the Chin Hills: 'The mere physical exertion of steering the wheel round the hairpin bends, apart from the shock of sudden stops and starts on the knife-edge precipices, with a drop of 1,000 feet over the side, was a terrible strain on nerves. We trickled along the passes at a rate of five miles an hour, if lucky.'

98

Beaton described Calcutta as 'a sort of oriental Clapham Junction' and its contrasts appalled him: 'Only fifteen paces from the main thoroughfare, opposite the most elegant European hotels, village-like groups are clustered around the fires, over which heavily spiced food and bits of fish are being fried in grease under the trees, while hordes of rats scurry to and fro.'

103

This photograph of Sir Mizram Ismail was reproduced along with several of Beaton's portraits of the Indian nobility in *Vogue* in September 1944. Beaton had been most impressed by the Prime Minister – 'a man of Persian extraction who combines energy and business sense with a poetic love of beauty' – and by his achievement in organising and beautifying the city of Jaipur in Rajputana.

104

Richard Casey, later Lord Casey, had an unusually varied wartime career. He was Australian Minister in Washington from 1940 to 1942, Minister of State in the Middle East with a seat in the British War Cabinet from 1942 to 1943 and Governor of Bengal from 1944 to 1946.

106

This informal study of Admiral Mountbatten was taken at his temporary headquarters in Delhi in January 1944, three months after his arrival to take up his appointment as Supreme Allied Commander in South East Asia. Beaton noted that Mountbatten 'appeared to have impregnated his immediate entourage with his own robust brand of enthusiasm. In spite of all the difficulties he had encountered no glaze of disappointment was yet visible in his pale blue eyes. They twinkled with the delight of a boy who had just been given a Meccano for Christmas.'

110

Field Marshal Wavell, who had been appointed Viceroy of India in 1943, made a considerable impact on Beaton: 'No finer example could be found than that set by the Viceroy. He is a paragon of truthfulness and deliberate fairness, industriousness, executive efficiency and courage.'

111

One of several photographs of the leave camp on the Viceroy's estate at Simla reproduced in *The Sketch* on 3 May 1944. Lord Wavell had established this camp to enable the troops to rest and recuperate away from the jungle in the healthy hill climate of Simla.

112–13

In contrast to the nerve-racking jungle warfare on the Burma front, Beaton found that: 'Life on the North-West Frontier has changed very little since the Victorian age, when warfare was so well conducted as to seem comparatively civilized.'

116–21

This group of photographs is taken from Beaton's record of daily life in India, which formed the basis for his book *India* published in Bombay in 1945. In the preface Beaton wrote of his attempt to convey 'a little of the beauty and strength of India'.

123

Beaton's photographs were reproduced in many types of publication. On 22 September 1945 *Nursing Mirror* used this one to illustrate an article on training Indian nurses to deal with emergencies.

126–8, 130, 144, 146–7

These photographs of Pihu military training centre were taken during the British Military Mission's tour of the remoter provinces of Free China. The main role of the mission was to supply military advisers to the Chinese army, particularly for training in commando tactics. 'Although the average age of the troops was said to be twenty, most of them appeared to be boys,' wrote Beaton. 'According to the standards of a crack European regiment, some of the drill did not appear particularly precise, their uniforms were of a poor material, and their sandals of straw; yet these youths put up a magnificent performance.'

130

Beaton wrote of the feast provided by General Li Mo-an 'A relay of delicious foods, said to be aphrodisiacs, was put before us, including sharks' fins and syllabub, all served with a hundred frills and decorations.'

131

Of General Chennault Beaton wrote: 'With the passage of years, he has become a little deaf; his mouth is tight-bitten and turns down at the corners. His complexion, yellow, as if stained by walnut juice, is pitted with deep crevices, and the skin around the jaw and neck is as wrinkled as the leather of the poor quality windbreaker he wears with the Flying Tiger painted crudely on the pocket.' The 'Flying Tigers' was the nickname of the US Fourteenth Air Force which, commanded by Chennault, maintained Free China's only link with the West for much of the war by flying the dangerous route over the 'Hump' from Calcutta to Chungking.

133

The Chinese nationalist party, the Kuomintang, which was founded in 1891 by Sun Yat-sen, was notoriously corrupt and ineffective. Beaton wrote: 'It did not take me many weeks to realise, when many allowances are made, that conditions are actually worse than they need be, and, that there might be some justification for the serious accusations that one hears about the corruption, dishonesty and "squeeze" employed in the running of the country and the conduct of the war.'

132

Beaton particularly admired Madam Sun Yat-sen: 'In a country where to be outspoken is sometimes dangerous, she does not hide her disappointment at the distance she believes the Government has travelled from the principles laid down by her husband, the Father of the Republic.'

134

The Belgian-born General Carton de Wiart was one of the few foreigners to be awarded the Victoria Cross. 'Although,' Beaton wrote, 'no English blood runs in his veins his appearance and manner are those of the traditional English warrior. With only one arm, the Victoria Cross and, he says, very few brains, he is an adventurer in the grand manner.' His brand of individual heroism appealed to Winston Churchill, whom he represented in Chungking from 1943 to 1946.

137

Chengtu was the former capital of Szechwan province and a centre of ancient provincial culture. Beaton found it most congenial and took photographs enthusiastically. He wrote afterwards that he had gained 'an impression of what once I imagined China to be'.

157

Vogue published this photograph in July 1945 just before the atomic bomb was dropped on Hiroshima on 6 August. The universal appeal of the image of a mother with her sick child was used to reinforce the message that in order to call a halt to the suffering Japan must be quickly defeated.

The Photographs Division
of the Ministry of Information

The Ministry of Information was created by the government at the outbreak of the war in September 1939. Its main function was to present the government's case at home and overseas by all available means of publicity. It was also responsible for the censorship of the press and release of official news, the production of government films, the supervision of the BBC, the mounting of official publicity campaigns and the maintenance of public morale. It was modelled on a similar department set up in February 1918 under Lord Beaverbrook, though its powers and activities were much more extensive. The new ministry was at first the subject of much criticism and ridicule and was particularly unpopular with the press. It lacked firm direction, its organisation was confused and its policies were uncertain and often contradictory. The Ministry's effectiveness improved dramatically after the appointment in July 1941 of Brendan Bracken as Minister of Information and, later in the same year, of the distinguished barrister C J Radcliffe (later Lord Radcliffe) as Director-General. Both remained in post until 1945. Bracken, a successful publisher and businessman and a close friend of the Prime Minister, established excellent relations with Fleet Street and won new respect for the Ministry's work.

The internal structure of the Ministry changed several times in the course of the war but from the middle of 1941 its two dozen or so divisions were broadly arranged in five groups responsible for the following activities: Home Publicity, Home Intelligence and Films; Overseas Publicity, Religions and Broadcasting; News, Censorship and Photographs; Publications, Exhibitions and Publicity Campaigns; and Finance and Establishments. There was also a Commercial Relations Division and a General Division responsible for coordinating the Ministry's work.

The Photographs Division, previously a section of the General Division, was formed on 3 May 1940. Its role was to gather photographs covering every aspect of the war at home and abroad and to distribute them as widely as possible throughout the United Kingdom and overseas. Starting with a staff of forty, its activities expanded until eventually over 200 people were concerned with the handling of photographs during their passage through the various channels of the Ministry. The Division's Director was the energetic and capable Hugh Francis, who had served in the Ministry of Information during the First World War and had spent the intervening years in business as a senior executive with EMI.

The Photographs Division's responsibilities included government control of photography in the United Kingdom, censorship and distribution of photographs and, in a limited way, the taking and commissioning of some of the official photographs. At the outbreak of the war strict legislation was passed to control photography by the general public and the press in order to prevent information of military value falling into enemy hands. The private citizen was banned from carrying a camera in a public place; press photographers could obtain a special permit but had to apply to the military authorities to photograph areas or subjects under their control. Much controversy arose over the question of whether taking photographs of military equipment in public places constituted an offence. Eventually it was decided that it was not so much the taking of photographs that mattered as the manner of their publication. Thereafter the Ministry of Information was content to confine its role to censorship.

Censorship of photographs operated at several interlinked levels in the services, the government and the Ministry of Information. The Ministry battled against the reluctance of the services to disclose information. As late as 1944 it was complaining that because of over-cautious suppression of detail and delays by the military censors at Allied Supreme Headquarters in Europe it had not been able to distribute good photographs to the press quickly enough. Each of the services employed and controlled its own photographers, whose pictures were frequently the only source of official news of the war on its various battle fronts.

Normally the military censor in the field was the first to scrutinise official photographs before passing them to the Censorship Division at the Ministry. There a team of military and civil censors decided which photographs could be published and whether any sensitive details had to be suppressed. The prints were then passed to the Photographs Division for distribution. However, because of the frequent need for speed the two Divisions normally worked in very close cooperation. Two copies of each photograph were submitted – one to Censorship for its ruling and one to Photographs to assess its news value. Press photographs were submitted directly to the censors at the Ministry. Although it was not directly responsible for it, the Ministry was anxious to improve the work of the official photographers employed by the War Office, Admiralty and Air Ministry. In May 1942, for example, it compiled a set of instructions for the Army Film and Photographic Unit's Sergeant Photographers which encouraged them to follow the example of such famous illustrated magazines as *Life* and *Illustrated* by creating photographic feature stories. The photographers were reminded that their pictures would serve many important and different purposes.

In the United Kingdom official photographs were released through established press channels, upon which the Ministry relied heavily. Overseas the Ministry had established a network of special distribution outlets. At home official photographs were released through two associations of the leading photographic agencies: the British International Press Photographic Agencies (BIPPA) and the Photographic News Agencies (PNA), who worked with the press proprietors' organisation, the Newspaper and Periodical Emergency Council. The press and photographic agencies also circulated their own photographs, though on a somewhat smaller scale than in peacetime because of shortages of staff and materials.

The Ministry's own distribution service sent photographs by wire and air mail to press attachés and information officers in all Allied and neutral countries. These photographs, which included selected press pictures, were used in various forms of pictorial publicity including the Ministry's own books, pamphlets, periodicals, posters and exhibitions. In any one week the number of prints distributed from Britain could amount to between 10,000 and 30,000. Paper shortages and communications difficulties encouraged the Ministry to establish printing and distributing centres overseas. By 1942, for example, both photographs taken in the Middle East and those sent out from London could be printed and distributed in Cairo to meet local needs within a vast area embracing the Middle East, Australia, Africa and the Far East.

In addition to these services the Division allowed the press and the public to use its growing library of photographs for research. It expected to deal with an average of 200 enquiries a week, ranging from those of authors writing about past campaigns to personal enquiries from the relatives of servicemen. It also operated a special lending library of 75,000 exhibition prints on such themes as recruiting campaigns, Anglo-Soviet cooperation and National Savings, which was available for government publicity campaigns.

Although the Ministry had its own photographers and laboratories it only made direct arrangements to take photographs if it needed material the press or the services could not supply. Its laboratories, which employed fourteen printers, concentrated rather on the mass production of prints of the service and press pictures. However, the Ministry occasionally commissioned professional photographers to undertake special projects. Bill Brandt's famous series of photographs of life in underground shelters during the London Blitz, which was taken for the Ministry of Home Security, came about in this way.

Later, the Ministry recruited its own small staff to improve its coverage of the home front and eventually by 1944 it employed five former press photographers – Jack Smith, Jack Bryson, Richard Stone, Norman Smith and Eric Joysmith – for this type of work. The range of subjects they were assigned was, nevertheless, very broad. In a typical week in January 1944 Jack Bryson took photographs of a new rehabilitation centre for wounded servicemen in London, recorded the arrival of some scarce sponges from Turkey, took some portrait shots at the Foreign Office of visiting diplomats and photographed the Surrey docks for the Ministry of Supply. By contrast, the terms of Cecil Beaton's employment were quite different. His post as Special Photographer was much more senior and his salary considerably higher. He reported personally to the Director, Hugh Francis, and enjoyed much greater freedom to select his subjects. He was the only photographer on the Ministry's staff to be sent abroad and the only official photographer to publish his photographs and accounts of his experiences in his own books during the war.

By 1946 the Ministry of Information had acquired comprehensive collections of photographs covering every aspect of the Second World War. These, together with the libraries compiled by the services departments, amounted to some two million photographs. In 1946 it was decided that this valuable historical record should be transferred to the Imperial War Museum and permanently preserved there. The transfer, which took five years to complete, followed a precedent set at the end of the First World War when the Museum received all the official photographs of that conflict. The Imperial War Museum's collections now contain some five million official, press and private photographs from Allied and enemy sources, illustrating almost every aspect of the two world wars and the other operations in which British and Commonwealth forces have been involved since August 1914.

The Collections

During the Second World War Cecil Beaton took approximately 10,000 photographs for the Ministry of Information, the largest body of work carried out for it by a single photographer. These photographs are now preserved in the collections of the Imperial War Museum and Sotheby's Belgravia.

The collection held at the Imperial War Museum comprises 6,939 photographs, the bulk of his wartime work. Most of these pictures were taken during his visits to the Middle East, India, Burma and China. Beaton normally returned his unprocessed 120 size films to the Ministry in London, which arranged for them to be developed and printed. The Ministry retained the negatives – all 2¼ inches square – which were filed in two series: 1,853 taken in the Middle East in 1942, and 4,548 taken in 1944 in India and China. All these photographs were transferred to the Imperial War Museum in 1946 with the Ministry of Information's Second World War Photographs Library. In addition the Museum received 326 negatives of Beaton's photographs of British shipyards and of the Royal Air Force, together with 212 prints made on the heavyweight matt paper he favoured. The photographs were accompanied by official Ministry captions based on information which Cecil Beaton supplied. Subsequently the Museum has made prints from all the negatives in its care. This collection may be consulted by members of the public in the Museum's Department of Photographs.

Beaton kept most of the negatives – some 3,000 in all – of the official photographs he took on the home front in 1940 and 1941. They were acquired by Sotheby's Belgravia in 1977 when Beaton sold his personal photographic collection to this famous auction house. The negatives will be preserved there as an archive of his work.

Books by Cecil Beaton
about the War Years

History under Fire: 52 Photographs of Air Raid Damage to London Buildings 1940–1
with a commentary by James Pope-Hennessy
London, Batsford, May 1941

Time Exposure: With a commentary and captions by Peter Quennell
London, Batsford, May 1941

Air of Glory: A Wartime Scrapbook
London, HMSO, 1941 (Issued by the Ministry of Information)

Winged Squadrons, London, Hutchinson, 1942

Near East, London, Batsford, 1943

Far East, London, Batsford, 1945

India, Bombay, Thacker, 1945

An Indian Album, London, Batsford, winter 1945–6

Chinese Album, London, Batsford, winter 1945–6

Photobiography, New York, Doubleday, 1951

The Years Between: Diaries 1939–44, London, Weidenfeld and Nicolson, 1965